John R Everhart

**By Boat and Rail**

John R Everhart

**By Boat and Rail**

ISBN/EAN: 9783337413088

Printed in Europe, USA, Canada, Australia, Japan

Cover: Foto ©Andreas Hilbeck / pixelio.de

More available books at **www.hansebooks.com**

# BY BOAT AND RAIL

BY

JOHN R. EVERHART, M.D.

G. P. PUTNAM'S SONS
NEW YORK      LONDON
27 West Twenty-third St.      24 Bedford St., Strand
The Knickerbocker Press
1892

COPYRIGHT, 1891
BY
JOHN R. EVERHART

Printed and Bound by
The Knickerbocker Press, New York
G. P. PUTNAM'S SONS

TO

R. J. BAILY, M.D.

WHO HAS BEEN MY COMPANION ON MANY A LONG JOURNEY
THIS VOLUME IS RESPECTFULLY
DEDICATED

# CONTENTS.

### CHAPTER I.
ARRIVAL IN GLASGOW—CUSTOM-HOUSE OFFICIALS—LOCH LOMOND—LOCH KATRINE . . . . 1-4

### CHAPTER II.
EDINBURGH—HOLYROOD PALACE—EDINBURGH CASTLE—SCOTT'S MONUMENT—THE BREWERIES . . . 5-8

### CHAPTER III.
MELROSE ABBEY—ABBOTSFORD—THE HIGHLANDS—THE STOCK—INTO ENGLAND . . . . 9-12

### CHAPTER IV.
LONDON—ST. PAUL'S—THE TOWER—THE POOR—CHARACTERISTICS OF THE ENGLISH PEOPLE—THE COCKNEY—THE WOMEN . . . . . 13-19

### CHAPTER V.
IN FRANCE — THE PEASANTRY — PARIS AND HER PEOPLE—THE RAG-PICKER AND THE RAT-CATCHER. 20-26

### CHAPTER VI.
PARIS—THE AMUSEMENTS—THE MORGUE—THE HOSPITALS AND SISTERS OF CHARITY—THE GUILLOTINE, 27-31

### CHAPTER VII.
PARIS—THE FRENCH MILITARY—THE EMPEROR—HIS POPULARITY AND DECLINE—FRENCH POLITENESS. 32-37

## CHAPTER VIII.

PARIS—THE TUILERIES—HÔTEL DES INVALIDES—LAFAYETTE'S GRAVE . . . . . . 38-41

## CHAPTER IX.

SPAIN—A BACKWARD COUNTRY—VALLADOLID—MADRID—THE ROYAL STABLES—THE ESCURIAL . 42-46

## CHAPTER X.

SPAIN—ZARAGOZA; ITS HEROIC DEFENCE—BARCELONA—THE FIRST STEAMBOAT—THE SPANISH PEOPLE. 47-52

## CHAPTER XI.

ALGIERS—ITS ANTIQUITY AND PIRATES—THE CUSTOMS OF THE PEOPLE—THE FRENCH MASTERS—THE PRODUCTS . . . . . . . 53-57

## CHAPTER XII.

MARSEILLES—THE CHÂTEAU D'IF—MONTE CARLO; ITS FAMOUS CASINO—THE CARNIVAL AT NICE. 58-63

## CHAPTER XIII.

GENOA—ITS PALACES AND HEROIC SIEGE BY MASSENA—PISA AND THE LEANING TOWER . . . 64-67

## CHAPTER XIV.

NAPLES AND ITS HISTORICAL PLACES—MT. VESUVIUS—POMPEII AND HERCULANEUM—THE TOMB OF VIRGIL—IMAGE-MAKING . . . . . 68-75

## CHAPTER XV.

ROME—ITS CHURCHES, TOMBS, RELICS—THE POPE—THE IMPROVED CONDITION OF THE CITY—THE PEASANTS—CURIOUS CUSTOMS . . . . 76-83

## Contents.

### CHAPTER XVI.

FLORENCE—ITS BEAUTIFUL STATUARY—BOLOGNA AND THE UNIVERSITY—THE CLOVER—MANTUA AND ITS MOATS . . . . . . . . 84–87

### CHAPTER XVII.

VENICE—ITS STREETS OF WATER—THE RIALTO AND ST. MARK'S—BEAD-MAKING—THE BRONZE HORSES OF ST. MARK'S . . . . . . 88–92

### CHAPTER XVIII.

AUSTRIA—TRIESTE AND ITS MIXED POPULATION—VIENNA—THE IMPERIAL COACH HOUSE—THE RELICS IN THE MUSEUM—THE SCHÖNBRUNN—NAPOLEON I. AND THE KING OF ROME . . . . . 93–96

### CHAPTER XIX.

FROM VIENNA TO BERLIN—PRAGUE AND ITS UNIVERSITY—DRESDEN AND ITS RELICS—BERLIN—NO IGNORANCE AND ALL SOLDIERS—EXCELLENT SANITARY LAWS . . . . . . . . 97–99

### CHAPTER XX.

LEIPSIC — THE FAMOUS "BATTLE OF NATIONS" FOUGHT ON ITS PLAINS—THE DUNGEONS OF RATISBON—MILAN TO TURIN—THROUGH THE MT. CENIS TUNNEL . . . . . . . . 100–103

### CHAPTER XXI.

GENEVA, THE CITY OF REFUGE FOR KNOX AND CALVIN—NO BEGGARS ALLOWED—VEVAY AND LAUSANNE . . . . . . . . 104–106

### CHAPTER XXII.

MT. BLANC—THE MER-DE-GLACE; ITS GRANDEUR—BERNE; ITS ORIGIN—THE BEAR-PIT . . 107–109

## CHAPTER XXIII.

IN ENGLAND AGAIN—CHESTER AND ITS SIGHTS—
ACROSS THE IRISH SEA TO BELFAST—DUBLIN AND
ITS CASTLE—HEROIC MONUMENTS—PARK AND
BREWERY . . . . . . . . 110–117

## CHAPTER XXIV.

CORK—OLD KINSALE AND ITS DANGEROUS ROCK
—THE LAKES OF KILLARNEY—HOMEWARD
BOUND . . . . . . . . 118–121

## CHAPTER XXV.

TO CALIFORNIA—SALT LAKE CITY—THE MORMONS—
THE TABERNACLE, THE TEMPLE, AND THE TITHING
HOUSE—SALT LAKE . . . . . . 122–126

## CHAPTER XXVI.

EN ROUTE FOR YOSEMITE VALLEY—ITS WONDERFUL
PEAKS AND WATERFALLS—CURIOUS CUSTOM OF THE
INDIANS—BIG TREES OF CALAVERAS . . 127–132

## CHAPTER XXVII.

SAN FRANCISCO—THE FAMOUS LICK OBSERVATORY—
THE CHINESE—OFF FOR PANAMA—CALLS AT MEXICAN PORTS—PANAMA—THE PIRATE MORGAN—BACK
TO NEW YORK . . . . . . . 133–138

## CHAPTER XXVIII.

AGAIN ACROSS THE CONTINENT—DENVER—VETA PASS
AND THE MULE SHOE—SANTA FÉ—SOUTHERN PACIFIC ROUTE—"KING OF THE COW-BOYS"—TUCSON
AND YUMA . . . . . . . 139–145

## CHAPTER XXIX.

LOS ANGELES—SANTA MONICA—MONTEREY—SANTA
CLARA VALLEY—AGAIN IN SAN FRANCISCO . 146-149

## CHAPTER XXX.

PRINCE EDWARD ISLAND—SHARP BURGLARS—TROUT
AND MACKEREL FISHING — WHITE MOUNTAINS —
SUMMIT OF MT. WASHINGTON . . . . 150-154

## CHAPTER XXXI.

QUEBEC, THE GIBRALTAR OF AMERICA—THE FALLS
OF MONTMORENCY — MONTREAL — THE THOUSAND
ISLANDS—THE CANADIAN PACIFIC RAILROAD—VIC-
TORIA—VANCOUVER ISLAND . . . . 155-162

## CHAPTER XXXII.

FROM VICTORIA TO ALASKA—FORT WRANGELL—CHIL-
KAHT INLET—THE MUIR GLACIER—SITKA—CURIOUS
CUSTOMS OF THE INDIANS — THE RETURN — THE
FOURTH OF JULY AT FORT WRANGELL—VICTORIA
AND SAN FRANCISCO . . . . . 163-173

## CHAPTER XXXIII.

FROM SAN FRANCISCO TO PORTLAND, OREGON — A
STAGE RIDE — THE SACRAMENTO VALLEY — ALONG
COLUMBIA RIVER TO WALLA WALLA AND TO SPO-
KANE—INTO THE NATIONAL PARK ; ITS GEYSERS,
CASCADES, AND MOUNTAINS—FROM THE PARK TO
THE GREAT LAKES—THE FAMOUS "SAULT" TO
NIAGARA . . . . . . . . 174-179

## CHAPTER XXXIV.

JACKSONVILLE, FLORIDA — THE BAHAMA ISLANDS —
NASSAU—REMINISCENCES OF "BLACKBEARD" . 180-189

## Contents.

### CHAPTER XXXV.

HAVANA—ITS ATTRACTIONS—STORY OF THE PIRATE MARTI—THE *Volante*—COWS MILKED AT THE DOOR . . . . . . . . 190–193

### CHAPTER XXXVI.

MATANZAS—CAVES OF BELLAMAR—RETURN TO HAVANA—DEPARTURE—OFF FOR MEXICO—PROGRESSO, YUCATAN—VERA CRUZ—FROM THE COAST TO THE CITY OF MEXICO . . . . . . 194–200

### CHAPTER XXXVII.

CITY OF MEXICO—THE NATIONAL DRINK—SUPERSTITION OF THE PEOPLE—THE OLD AQUEDUCT—RELICS OF THE AZTECS AND TOLTECS—HABITS OF THE PEOPLE—CHAPULTEPEC—A BULL-FIGHT . . 201–209

### CHAPTER XXXVIII.

UP THE MISSISSIPPI—NEW ORLEANS—A FLOOD IN THE "FATHER OF WATERS" . . . . . 210–212

### CHAPTER XXXIX.

BOUND FOR SOUTH AMERICA—ST. THOMAS—THE AMAZON—PARA—PERNAMBUCO AND BAHIA—THEIR EXPORTS AND CUSTOMS . . . . . 213–220

### CHAPTER XL.

RIO JANEIRO—ITS BEAUTIFUL HARBOR—ITS STREETS AND SQUARES—CURIOUS SHOPS—PETROPOLIS—COFFEE GROWING AND MODE OF TRANSPORTATION—STINGLESS BEES . . . . . . 221–227

### CHAPTER XLI.

THE BERMUDA ISLANDS—THE TREES AND BIRDS—MANNER OF HOUSE BUILDING—SCARCITY OF WATER—PLACES OF NOTE—THE DOCKYARDS—HOMEWARD BOUND AND STORM AT SEA . . . . 228–233

# BY BOAT AND RAIL.

## CHAPTER I.

THE first indication to the traveller of his approach to the shores of the Old World is the appearance of a long smoky line in the distance, which to the untrained eye resembles a cloud. A surer sign, however, is the transformation of the passengers from their old to their new clothing; also, the rapid removal of contraband articles from trunks to places of greater security. The lover of tobacco steps ashore with his boots, hat, and mouth crammed with the popular narcotic.

As our vessel steamed up the narrow Clyde to Glasgow through a fleet of boats, the passengers rejoiced that the monotonous ocean had been traversed; while the race-horses on board, bruised and sickened by the voyage, neighed at the sight of the green hills and fresh clover of Scotland. These unfortunate animals, as the result showed, made better sailors than runners at the Derby, for they retained their sea-legs even on the turf.

At the custom-house the officials were polite and often convivial, even permitting you to smell the aroma of your own cigars while they smoked them. Landing safely at Glasgow, and pushing our way through the multitude of drays and cabs which lined the wharf, we at last arrived at the hotel, and, shaking hands with a dandy waiter, whom we mistook for the proprietor, we were shown to a room for which five dollars a day was charged, which had the effect of leading one to think that his entertainment would be luxurious, but his departure sudden.

The straight streets, the tall, granite houses, without window-shutters, the factories with the tallest chimneys in the world—one of which is four hundred and thirty feet high,—the hum of trade, and the rapid movement of the people indicate that Glasgow is a commercial city. In population it ranks third in the United Kingdom.

## By Boat and Rail. 3

It is one of the greatest shipbuilding ports in the world. Here in the early years of the present century the first steamboat was built. To-day the Clyde vessels can be seen in nearly every harbor, and sailing upon all navigable waters. In this city the printing of calicoes and steam spinning machinery were first introduced.

Leaving the dust and smoke of the town for the more genial air of the country, we went to Loch Lomond, the largest lake in Scotland. It is a beautiful body of water, dotted with a number of picturesque islands. The shore is precipitous, from which rivulets tumble into the placid lake; while here and there are green vales, on which shepherds and their dogs watch browsing flocks.

Towering above the loch, in majestic grandeur, is Ben Lomond, thirty-two hundred feet high. We tramped through the tangled grass, over sharp stones, scaring the hare from the heather, and climbing the mountain until the hawk circled below. In the distance were seen the Atlantic Ocean, the Highlands pencilled against the sky, and far to the east lay Edinburgh.

Loch Katrine, the scene of the *Lady of the Lake*, is separated from Loch Lomond by a glen. This glen was the home and haunt of Rob Roy, and his cave is still pointed out. Loch Katrine is the most famous lake in Scotland, and is the source of the water supply of Glasgow, twenty-five miles distant. From Glasgow we went to Edinburgh, through an attractive and agricultural country—

> " With herds the pastures thronged,
> With flocks the hills."

## CHAPTER II.

EDINBURGH, which Ben Jonson recognized by its odor, when he said—

"Sweet Edinburgh, I smell thee now,"

has undergone considerable change in the way of purification since his time; yet it still savors of its ancient quality, for,

"Like the vase in which roses have once been distilled—
You may break, you may shatter the vase if you will,
But the scent of the roses will hang round it still."

This city, surrounded by fortified hills, and abounding in rich architectural monuments, stands eminent as a seat of science and learning among the cities of the world. The stranger is surprised at the striking difference between the old town and the new; the former with its houses twelve and thirteen stories high, black with the smoke of centuries, with its narrow closes like burrows, is filled with the poor; while the latter is distinguished by its fine houses and wide streets, thronged with trade and fashion. Here can be seen the Highlander, with his tartan plaid and bagpipe, proud of his national costume and his discordant music.

The city is filled with curiosities and historical associations. In Holyrood Palace, which was the ancient residence of the Scottish kings and queens, the visitor is shown the bedchamber of the beautiful but unfortunate Mary Queen of Scots, which remains as it was when she occupied it. The blood of the ill-fated Rizzio still stains the floor, and the bed of Charles I. reminds one of that fated king. The immense galleries are lined with the portraits of the one hundred and six kings of Scotland, and the bones of some of them are mouldering in the vaults of the chapel.

The Cathedral of St. Giles is a venerable structure, at one time having forty altars within its walls. In the cemetery adjoining are the ashes of John Knox, the ecclesiastical reformer. His house still stands, with this inscription over the door, "Love thy neighbor as thyself."

Edinburgh Castle, next to Holyrood, is the most prominent and interesting place in the city. Here may be seen portions of that enormous piece of ordnance, called "Mons Meg," made by a country blacksmith, assisted by his wife, who blew the bellows. This gun was made in 1486, the bore being twenty inches in diameter. In the castle are preserved the ancient crown, the sword of state, and other regalia of Scotland.

In proximity to the castle is the museum, in which is the skeleton of the murderer Burke, who strangled about a score of persons merely for the purpose of selling their bodies.

Near the city is Arthur's Seat, a hill eight hundred feet high, named in honor of King Arthur. The upper portion of the hill is formed of columns of basalt, which are called "Samson's Ribs." From the summit of this elevation there is presented a magnificent panorama of the surrounding country.

On Prince's Street is a monument to the memory of Sir Walter Scott, a beautiful tribute by a native artist, and built like a steeple resting upon the ground. On top of Calton Hill is a monument of Lord Nelson.

Edinburgh, the "Hub of Scotland," contains a university, founded over three hundred years ago, celebrated both in the United Kingdom and abroad. Here can be pursued a full university course, either of theology, medicine, and law, or the arts and sciences. The library contains over one hundred and fifty thousand volumes. There is also a complete anatomical museum and a botanical garden attached to the university.

The "new town" is connected with the old by Dean Bridge, which spans the river Leith. It is one hundred feet above the stream, and nearly the same in length. One of the oldest industries of the city is that of ale and beer brewing. There are thirty breweries, which consume annually nearly a million bushels of malt. The Scotch are economical and penurious, and Jews are scarce, because they cannot compete with them in driving a bargain.

## CHAPTER III.

A RIDE of a half hour on the cars brings you to Melrose Abbey, where the guide will explain the wonders of the place in such broad Scotch, that one is none the wiser after his harangue is finished. Melrose Abbey was founded by King David I., in 1136. Now it is deserted, and the sparrows may be seen feeding their young in the outstretched hands of the Apostles, who stand in the niches of the ivy-covered walls. The workmanship of the abbey is so exquisite that the fibre of the flowers can still be traced on the chiselled ruins, which have been marred by time and Cromwell's cannon. Here also is the stone upon which Sir Walter Scott was accustomed to sit and meditate among the graves of his ancestors.

In the abbey is the sepulchre of Alexander III., and a silver urn containing the heart of the great Bruce. Wandering among the foot-worn epitaphs and the moss-covered slabs, one can see some curious inscriptions, as " Here lies the body of an honest man "; which argues that Diogenes with his lantern never visited the neighborhood of Melrose.

About three miles from the abbey is Abbotsford, the home of Scott; in front flows the Tweed, while the hills and woods hide it from the public view. At the gate we met the old game-keeper, with a brace of rabbits, who delights in showing the visitor over the house. Here is Scott's chair; his Highland kilt, the last he wore; the gun of Rob Roy; the pistols of Napoleon; and a library of twenty thousand volumes.

Six miles from Abbotsford is Dryburgh Abbey, where the great author of the *Waverley Novels* is buried. It is an old building, built after the architecture of the twelfth century.

As we left this region of poetry, song, and romance, the long shadows told that evening was approaching. The setting sun gilded the Selkirk hills, the linnet was singing in the hawthorne, the cattle were lowing in the meadow, and the milk-maid's song mingled with the strains of the shepherd's pipe.

The Scotch are honest and devoted to their religion; but some of them are neither too clean nor too sober, being rather extravagant in the use of whiskey and sparing in the application of water. The police are vigilant on the Sabbath, and fail not to remind the whistler or musician of the sanctity of the day.

From Edinburgh to London the route was via Liverpool, and through the Highlands, which at this season of the year (mid-spring) were beautiful. On the way we stopped overnight at a highland village for the purpose of enjoying the scenery. The dark mountains in the distance, the emerald valley, the white blossom of the hawthorne, the warbling of the skylark, and the murmuring of the falling water made us realize how true it is that "God made the country, and man made the town." In Scotland every inch of arable ground is under cultivation, and the hedge fences are cut as nicely and as carefully as a barber would trim the hair.

Just before crossing into England we passed through Gretna Green, a town that has been made famous as the resort of English lovers, who, in order to evade the English marriage laws, resorted thither to a blacksmith who acted as priest. On the route we noticed a number of Holstein cattle, although Durhams and Alderneys were the most common. The sheep were large, resembling animated bales of cotton. The horses appeared unusually fine both in size and in general appearance. The highways were kept in excellent condition. The first macadamized road was constructed here, so called from Macadam, the originator.

In due time our train carried us into Liverpool, a city of ships, like ancient Tyre, where every one appeared by their haste to have just arrived or about to leave. After a few hours we resumed our journey towards London. The cars were of the usual character, uncomfortable and crowded; consequently, when an Englishman stumbles into the stuffy little car, with his bundle of umbrellas and canes, his bags, and blankets, and his feet, the space and conversation become correspondingly limited.

The route passed through a rich and fertile district, covered with systematic farms and improved stock. The train ran at a continuous speed of fifty miles an hour. We noted the incessant whistle of the locomotive, the numerous straggling houses, the long line of standing cars, and at last the dense cloud of smoke which always hangs over the capital of the British Empire.

## CHAPTER IV.

THE first object that strikes the eye is the dome of the Cathedral of St. Paul, which is the largest Protestant church in the world. It is a Gothic edifice covering over two acres of ground. The height to the top of the cross is four hundred and four feet. The cross itself is thirty feet high, and the ball on the steeple will hold ten or a dozen persons. The two dials of the clock, one south, the other west, are twenty feet in diameter. The minute-hands are ten feet in length, and weigh seventy-five pounds each; the hour-hands are six feet in length and weigh forty-four pounds each. The figures are two feet long. The great bell is ten feet in diameter, weighing nearly twelve thousand pounds, and its sound can be heard at the distance of twenty-five miles. From the ball one looks down upon the moving mass of men and horses, which have the appearance of insects, but the everlasting roar of London scarcely reaches the ear. Half-way down the dome is the whispering gallery, which is so constructed that persons over one hundred feet apart can hold a conversation in a whisper.

In the crypt, Wellington, the Iron Duke; Lord Cornwallis, of Yorktown fame; and Lord Nelson, the hero of Trafalgar and Copenhagen, are buried. Here also, Benjamin West, the painter, who was born in Delaware County, Pa., lies entombed among the great men of England. Over the entrance of the choir is this brief inscription: "Here beneath lies Christopher Wren, builder of this church and city, who lived more than ninety years, not for his own, but the public good. Reader! if you seek his monument, look around you!"

After viewing the Cathedral, we boarded one of the little steamers which ply upon the Thames, which does not smell in the least like the "apples of Solomon," and in a short time we were landed at the Tower of London, which was founded by William the Conqueror. It has been a palace, a place of refuge, and a prison, but now it is an exhibition building from which the government receives a sixpence from each visitor. Here one is shown by a guide the Bloody Tower, where Richard III. murdered his two nephews, the spot where Henry VI. was assassinated, and the room where the Duke of Clarence was drowned in a butt of Malmsey wine. In the Brick Tower is the execution block, stained with the blood of Mary Queen of Scots and of Lady Jane Grey. In another room are the gilded armors of the ancient kings, and guns, like Colt's revolvers, made centuries ago. In a building, constructed especially for the purpose, the crown jewels, regalia, and sceptre are kept.

Not far from here is the Thames Tunnel, formerly a footway under the river, but now used as a railway.

The immensity of London is marvellous. Through its innumerable streets over five million people swarm, gaining a livelihood, God only knows how!

The famous London docks cover many acres, and adjoining are the vaults, where over a hundred thousand pipes of wine are stored.

The Strand is one of the most crowded thoroughfares, where pickpockets are as plentiful as fleas in Rome, and where money is even safer in the bank than in the pocket.

The numerous hospitals are supplied with able corps of physicians and surgeons, and with everything that surgical ingenuity can invent.

We wandered through Westminster Abbey, which is over six centuries old, and was built by Henry III., who dedicated it to the worship of God; although now it is entered more from curiosity than for prayer. Art has garnished it with her noblest works, and patriotism has consecrated it to the repose of heroes, poets, and kings.

In London may be found the richest and the poorest people under the sun. In it you can get more for a shilling and less for a pound than in any other place. Here may be seen many a sore, ragged, and hungry Lazarus, waiting "for the crumbs which may fall from the rich man's table." In one part of the city, where crime and poverty are rife, lodgings and board for a day can be had for "tuppence ha'-penny"; but the knives and forks are chained to the table, to remind the rather unscrupulous guest that these utensils are not included in the bill of fare.

The English people are brave, generous, stubborn, haughty, conceited, and suspicious. They are slow thinkers and good feeders, never dying in debt to their stomachs. They delight in all kinds of fancy sports, from a chicken fight to a contest in the prize-ring. They are at home on the turf, for which they abandon all kinds of business, and bet all sorts of sums on their favorites. Their jockeys are as famous as their politicians, and for one of them to gain the inside track occasions more applause than a majority vote in Parliament. The Derby attracts immense crowds, who go in all kinds of conveyances. The four-in-hand, double, tandem, and single teams, and steam are brought into requisition to convey prince and peasant to the same destination. Parliament and the courts adjourn for the Derby, which is a national holiday. There is good order on the grounds, and when the racing is over the human race starts for the cars, and he is lucky who succeeds in procuring transportation.

Another amusement is the Mock Court, where the judge, dressed in wig and gown, *charges* his glass with more skill than he does the jury, and where the limbs of the law, seedy with justice, are so well *read* that they show it even in the ends of their noses.

The cockney is a curiosity. He praises his country a little too much. He thinks that there is nothing worth seeing or knowing outside of London, and boasts that his government is the best, equally lauding the dexterity of his thieves and the eloquence of his bishops. He does not forget the flavor of his "heggs" and "'ams," nor the swiftness of his "'orses" and "'ounds." He seldom goes out of the sound of Bow Bells, or out of the sight of St. Paul's. One of them, who had ventured into the country for a day's shooting, on being told that a hare was approaching, exhibited his bravery and knowledge of natural history by saying, "Let 'im come, hi fear 'im not."

The English women are the prettiest in the world, with the exception of our own. They are beautiful because they are healthy, owing to their heavy shoes, comfortable clothing, beefsteaks, ale, and exercise. They are also resolute and strong. We have seen them riding the mustang over the Sierra Nevada Mountains and through the Yosemite Valley, or trudging up the abrupt sides of Mount Vesuvius through lava and cinders, or scudding a gondola through the streets of Venice, or on horseback on their own native heath, clearing hedges and ditches "with locks thrown back and lips apart," their cheeks glowing with excitement "as the deer sweeps by and the hounds are in full cry, and the hunter's horn is ringing."

But England, with all her antipathies and prejudices, is true to herself, and when we left her "pale and white-faced shore," it was not without regret, for Englishmen are generous foes and faithful friends.

## CHAPTER V.

FROM London we went to Dover, where we took the boat for France, and after crossing the English Channel, a ride of a few hours, we landed at Calais. Here the customhouse officials in uniforms examined our baggage. They knew enough English to ask for our passports and to wish us a good voyage.

After some little excitement and anxiety at the railway station, as to whether ourselves and baggage would reach the same destination, we were ushered by a guard into a room and locked in. When all was in readiness to move, the guard blew his horn, the doors were opened, and, without crowding as if life depended upon being the first to get a seat, the passengers reached the cars. They have accommodations for eight persons. As far as safety goes the tourist may feel content, for the railway system of Europe seems to be perfect. The road is enclosed by good fences, the public highways are protected by gates, and the bridges are properly guarded. Still the cars are not so comfortable as those in our own country.

The northern portion of France resembles the rolling prairie of our Western States; the farms have neither fences around them nor houses upon them. On an acre of ground there will be as many varieties of crops as there are patches in a bedquilt. The women and dogs act as substitutes for fences; the former tether the cattle with ropes attached to their horns, and the latter guard the flocks with watchful care. The people still cut grain with the old-fashioned sickle, and plough with a wheel fixed to the beam. The farmers live in villages called communes, instead of in isolated houses, for the Frenchman without company is as lonesome as a Dutchman without his pipe and lager.

The French peasantry are industrious and saving, without being penurious. The men wear beards, blouses, and wooden shoes; the women, attired in short dresses, have their hair twisted and secured with silver pins shaped like daggers, and their heads are partially covered with red handkerchiefs.

The trip between Calais and Paris occupies

but a few hours. The route is through a very highly cultivated country largely made up of trucking farms, the product of which goes almost exclusively to Paris to feed its multitudes. As the train approaches Paris there are certain unmistakable signs that point out the proximity of the magnificent capital of France. For miles along the railroad there are villas, small farms, and gardens rich with flowers; a portion of the city is traversed before the depot is reached. Here we stopped, and at the appearance of the guard, who released the passengers, we stepped forth into the most pretentious city of the world, the Mecca of all nations, and the wonder of all peoples. A few minutes later we were quartered in the Grand Hotel, which is one of the best in the city.

Paris is a charming place and immense sums of money have been lavished to render it beautiful and attractive, while improvements spring up every day. The visitor is fascinated by its artificial lakes, its splendid gardens, its long avenues, its tossing fountains, and merry crowds. The boulevards are as clean as a floor, lined with imposing buildings and stores filled with luxury and art. On the boulevards there are but few drays or heavy wagons; in their places are private carriages, coupés, and omnibuses with seats on top, a style that has been recently introduced into the cities of this country. The pavements are free from bales and boxes, and impetuous clerks do not make a reputation as business men by jostling those they meet. Gay cafés, with tables in front, are occupied by the fatigued and the idle, who sit and sip their black coffee mixed with brandy instead of cream. At these resorts may be observed the moving multitude, made up of all nationalities and costumes: the fat and florid Englishman, after his roast beef and "hale"; the lean, lank, and sallow Italian, living on conspiracies and macaroni; the heavily bearded nihilist, thinking of bombs and dynamite, and breathing forth destruction against the Czar; the white-robed Arab, the Indian of the desert; the square-headed but intellectual German, exhaling smoke and discussing metaphysics; the kilted Scotchman from beyond the Tweed; the prayerful Turk, with matted beard and eyes dreamy with opium; the coal-black African, like Shakespeare's breeze "stealing and giving odor"; the almond-eyed Chinaman, all cue and no eyebrows, on the lookout for rice and rat pie; the American, swinging along the streets with his hands in his pockets, recognized as a bonanza king; and women of all styles of beauty, with dresses as variegated as butterflies, and with high-heeled shoes clanking over the cemented pavements and keeping time to the music of their tongues.

The French modes are of such infinite variety, that there does not appear to be any set fashion. A bonnet over the nose, or one upon the neck, or a coat with a long or a short skirt, do not cause surprise. The dress of the women is of every style that pleases the fancy, and is worn more on account of its neatness than for ostentation. The women are admired for their grace, wit, and amiability, rather than for the flash of their jewels or the price of their robes.

One soon becomes accustomed to French manners, which are fascinating; to their black coffee, and to their drink of sugar and water, to which the native is partial. The French have but two meals a day, and their appetites are as good as their dishes.

## By Boat and Rail. 25

The immorality of Paris has become a byword, and perhaps the people deserve it; but still, "*Honi soit qui mal y pense.*" At least, they do not have improper lectures by charlatans who live on, while they laugh at, the simplicity of their patients, as in other countries; nor are skilful magicians permitted to make money and create diseases out of good pulses.

Among the occupations of the Parisians, that of the rag-picker is prominent, it being a business that is monopolized, because it affords a good margin on a small capital, since the pack-basket and iron-pointed stick are the only implements which are needed to turn rags into gold. Honest and industrious in his humble avocation, the rag-picker is always anxious for excitement. Some of them are the first in the revolution of fashions, prices, and thrones. Here is the *commissionaire*, who stands at the corner and, for a slight recompense, will do anything that eyes and ears can accomplish. Other professions are those of the dog-shaver and rat-catcher; the latter will not only slaughter rats, but, as his sign indicates, will enter the more dexterous arena and kill bed-bugs at ten sous an hour.

There is also the vendor of lemonade, who carries his beverage in a vessel upon his back, like a peddler, and, from the sparingness of the ingredients and the minuteness of the doses, proves that he is strong in the homœopathic faith; and on every street may be heard the loud-mouthed *marchand des habits*, proclaiming his occupation. There is a jealous aristocracy even among the scavengers. Their pride of birth is inveterate. Their social circles are distinct. The rag-picker's son turns up his nose at the rat-catcher's daughter.

Respectability in Paris does not depend so much on the manner of dress and living as it does in England. A gentleman may lodge in an attic, eat at a café, wear unfashionable clothing, and make a visit on foot. Wealth is considered important, but not essential to gentility. This is one of the social conventionalities of France, which might be adopted elsewhere with advantage.

## CHAPTER VI.

THE French seem intent on the pursuit of pleasure. They forsake their homes to seek amusement on the streets. They saunter through the Jardin des Plantes, noisy with the roar of wild beasts, screaming birds, and chattering monkeys, and luxuriant with vegetable life, "from the cedar tree of Lebanon even unto the hyssop that springeth out of the wall." They stroll around the fountains in the Place de la Concorde. They watch the children flying their painted balloons, feeding the pigeons from their hands, or launching their tiny boats among the lily-pads on the lakes in the Jardin des Tuileries. They stop to observe the military manœuvres in the Champ de Mars. They ramble among the shrubbery of Versailles, or through the shady avenues of Fontainebleau. They never tire of visiting the Louvre and the Palace of Luxembourg, where are galleries of paintings miles long, which illustrate, more clearly than books, the history, the tastes, and the genius of the people.

The French delight in dancing, feasting, and theatre-going. Their ball-rooms are supplied with confectionery, flowers, and all that pleases the eye. They have halls of all kinds, from the Hôtel de Ville, where the noblesse, flashing with diamonds, walk and bow through the dances, to the Château de Fleurs, where the student whirls his partner through the mazes of the can-can with the velocity of a spindle.

There are *fêtes* without number; the Emperor, and later the President, having his *fête* days as well as the *blanchisseuse*. When her holiday comes round she leaves her aquatic pursuits of soapsuds and soiled linen, and rides in procession through the streets, with water lilies in her hand as emblems of the purity of her trade.

At any time you may see crowds in the Champs Elysées shaking with laughter at the rough wit and antiquated jokes of the mountebanks.

On the banks of the Seine is a small building called the Morgue, where the unknown dead

## By Boat and Rail. 29

are exposed for three days, in order to be claimed by their friends. It is a proverbial fact that women never pass it without stopping, which shows that they have an anxiety for the dead as well as for the living. The hospital arrangements of Paris are perfect. A hundred of these charitable institutions are thrown open to the infirm and afflicted, and thousands of patients are annually admitted to their wards. The most die from consumption, and the fewest from *mania a potu*. These hospitals are handsomely supported by private contributions and legacies, and by a tax of ten per cent. on the receipts of all places of amusement. One admires the Sisters of Charity, who, secluded from the world, pass their lives amid contagion and death, and, as "ministering angels," day and night supply the wants of the sick, and console the dying; their gentleness and kindness have endeared them alike to patients and physicians, who address them by the tender sobriquet of "Mother." Here medical men from all parts of the world gather, eager to see the new and dexterous operations, and hear the latest theories of celebrated teachers. They crowd the halls, as did the students of old at the famous schools of Greece.

A desire to see everything that the capital offers, may lead the visitor to the place of execution to witness the operation of the guillotine, the national razor that shaves but once. Before Napoleon I. became Emperor it stood in the Place de la Concorde, which was then called the Place de la Révolution. By that instrument of death Louis XVI., Charlotte Corday, Marie Antoinette, Danton, Desmoulins, Robespierre, and twenty-eight hundred others were executed during the days of the Revolution. The guillotine is simple in construction, but terrible in action, and one realizes, with Voltaire, the ferocious curiosity of the people.

> " With barbarous haste, with tumult fierce and loud,
> Round the dire scaffold throng the curious crowd,
> They pant for blood and urge with furious breath,
> The destined hour to feast their eyes on death."

The victim appears, dressed in execution clothing, with his hands tied behind his back. As he steps upon the instrument, which is painted red to hide the blood, a spring throws him into the proper position, and like a flash the heavy knife drops from its height, the head leaps from the body, the warm blood gushes from the lifeless trunk, and a spasmodic shudder runs through the retiring crowd.

## CHAPTER VII.

THE French military under the Republic is not the gay and gaudy force that it was under the Empire, nor are there as many soldiers quartered in Paris. During our first visit the city was full of armed men, and yet the "Empire was Peace." Every tenth man was a soldier. Their uniforms were of such varied cuts and colors, that it seemed impossible to invent new ones. There was the warlike zouave, with red and white turban, Turkish trousers, blue jacket, forehead shaved, and beard of formal cut; the heavy-mounted gendarme, with bearskin hat and long top-boots; the light and swift huzzar; the picturesque lancer, with colors flying at the end of his spear; the quick-stepping *chasseur*, and the imperial guard, from whose ranks came the "bravest of the brave." In those imperial days, companies were marching all day long through the streets, to the rattle of the kettle-drum, or to the sound of the bugle. Frequently regiments were seen, headed by the drum-major, who, with lofty steps and savage air, flourished his silver-headed cane to time the music and awe the children; while the "daughter of the regiment," dressed in red bloomer, with canteen and sword, marched bravely, as if fearing neither war nor wine. Then came the veteran of a hundred battles, tottering along, enfeebled by age and wounds, having lost, perhaps, a limb, either among the burning sands of the Pyramids, or amid the everlasting snows of Russia, contrasting strongly with the dandy *cent-garde*, who on prancing steed and with golden spurs, slays only with his eyes.

Under the Empire not only the military but all government officials were uniformed. The six thousand policemen had no star to hide in case of a row, for their cocked hats and straight swords indicated their office. They were always ready to direct a stranger or to quell a fight. The streets are well lighted, and after dark, every vehicle, from a wheel-barrow to the imperial carriage, is compelled to carry a light, which not only tends to enliven the city, but its value is known by the scarcity of accidents.

In company with my friend, Gen. G. Pennypacker, we witnessed in the Champ de Mars, a review of sixty thousand men, equipped with all the accoutrements of war. The Emperor, with his military staff, inspected the different regiments while riding through the ranks. His graceful horsemanship attracted universal attention. Sometimes he stopped to decorate a private or pass a compliment upon an officer, while the cry of *Vive l'Empereur* rang along the line. There were sham fights, where the impetuous charge of cavalry shook the earth as they bore down upon the serrated ranks and hollow squares of infantry; while the shock of the huge mass of men and horse, the roar of cannon, rattle of musketry, the clanging of swords, and the clear sound of the zouave bugle above the noise and din recalled the terror and pomp of real war. When the smoke had vanished, the vast army was seen standing in perfect order, as if it had not moved.

At the time of our visit the Emperor was fifty-seven years old. His height was five feet, seven inches, his shoulders slightly rounded, his hands and feet small. His face was rather handsome, with a high forehead, a cunning and vicious eye, and a large and prominent nose ; a heavy moustache, waxed and pointed, covered his mouth, and an imperial adorned his chin. His head was round with the hair cut short, his expression calm and determined, his manner easy and graceful. This was the man that was a prisoner at the Fortress of Ham, an exile in America, a policeman in London, the President of the Republic, and then the Emperor, who, like his great uncle, became again a prisoner and an exile, and died upon English soil.

Napoleon III. was the most accomplished ruler of Europe and an excellent linguist, speaking six languages fluently. As an author, he wrote several works on military tactics and civil government. As an orator, he was eloquent, terse, and profound ; as a conversationalist, enticing, but preferring to listen rather than talk. His bravery and intrepidity were such that it is said he never changed a muscle of his face at the crack of the assassin's pistol ; and the crowd marvelled at his coolness and indifference when the infernal machines exploded at his feet. His bravery on the fields of Magenta and Solferino won to him the hearts of the soldiers and the plaudits of the nations.

Like Cæsar and Napoleon I., he believed in a "star of destiny," which superstitious confidence, in itself, was a source of popularity and safety. He flattered the army because it sustained him. The *bourgeois* preferred to endure him rather than risk a revolution. The peasants loved him for the traditionary lustre of his name.

The downfall of the Empire through the Franco-Prussian war was a great surprise to the world. It is said that Napoleon was opposed to the war at the outset, but he was forced into it by the people. After the surrender at Sedan he was imprisoned for several months at Wilhelmshöhe, and, on his release, he retired to England. During his imprisonment in German territory the Empire had been overthrown and a Republic declared.

The French, as a nation, are excitable, patriotic, brave, and polite. Their excitement has been too often exhibited in the bloody riots of Paris. The exile shows his patriotism by tears or enthusiasm at the mention of La Belle France, and his bravery is not questioned when the bridge of Lodi or trenches of Sebastopol are mentioned. Politeness is universal.

The men touch their hats when they enter a shop, and when they pass a funeral cortege or a church. They are prompt to apologize for a wrong, and, it is said, will scarcely resent an insult without an introduction. As Voltaire has said : " At times they either act like tigers or like monkeys."

## CHAPTER VIII.

AT every turn in Paris, palaces, churches, arches, and columns meet the eye. The Column de Vendôme is made from twelve hundred cannon taken from the Austrians and Russians by the great Napoleon. The Arc de Triomphe, grand in its conception and magnificent in its workmanship, is at the entrance of the Avenue des Champs Elysées. This monument was erected by Napoleon to commemorate the victories of himself and his marshals. The Palais des Tuileries, noble in its extent, modest in its architecture, luxuriantly furnished yet without ostentation, has been the residence of Catherine de Medici, Charles IX., Louis XIII., Louis XIV., and the Napoleons. The Cathedral of Notre-Dame, so old that its history is lost in obscurity, is still unfinished, and the rooks have built their nests in its moss-covered turrets. Whilst new shafts and spires were being completed, revolutions swept through it and robbed it of its treasures; even the coronation robes of Napoleon I. were not spared, and the leaden coffins that contained the remains of Louis XIII. and XIV. were melted into bullets by the infuriated mob.

The Hôtel des Invalides is a noble building, designed as a home for old soldiers. In the council-chamber are the portraits and busts of Napoleon and his marshals, and of some of the Bourbon kings. Under the dome lie the remains of the Great Emperor, who had desired in his will that his ashes should repose on the banks of the Seine, among the French people, whom he loved so well. In this hotel a home was given to the "Old Guard," whose motto was "to die but never surrender." Only recently one might have seen some of these old "heroes of a hundred battles" reverently standing and pressing their gray moustaches against the iron bars of their Emperor's tomb, with tears rolling down their scarred and sabre-cut faces, as they recalled the "Little Corporal," the Grand Emperor, and the Exile's dust.

Americans should not leave Paris without visiting the grave of Lafayette. In an obscure part of the city, in the Rue de Picpus, No. 15, at the extremity of the Faubourg St. Antoine, is the family burying-ground of the Lafayettes and of some old noble families, which is surrounded by walls forming an oblong enclosure. On the southeast angle is a plain black slab, and beneath it lies that great and good man, the friend of Washington, and the hero of the battle of the Brandywine. On the occasion of his funeral, Dr. Cloquet, author of the *Recollections of Lafayette*, said: "No speeches were pronounced over the General's grave. After the usual prayers, the earth sent by your countrymen from America was mingled with that of France, to encircle and protect all that was left of Lafayette." By his side repose the remains of his son, George Washington Lafayette. What a contrast between his modest resting-place and some of those in the cemetery of Père la Chaise, whose inmates are only remarkable for the grandeur that covers them! Or, compare his grave with those of the kings in the Church of St. Denis, where the light streams through the stained glass of the Gothic windows, and the heavy sound of the deep-toned organ shakes the very dust in their golden coffins. When you read the simple epitaph, "LAFAYETTE," whose life was associated with so much patriotism, chivalry, and misfortune, you recall the Revolution of Paris, the prison of Olmutz, and the green hills and hospitable homes of the Brandywine. As long as that stream shall flow through luxuriant meadows, enriched by his blood, and as long as harvests shall wave over the trophies of that struggle in which he shared and labored, as long as prosperity and genius shall bloom beneath the shelter of this glorious Union, whose mighty arch he helped to rear, so long will the American people cherish and revere the name of Lafayette !

## CHAPTER IX.

THE trip from Paris to Madrid, by way of Tours and Bordeaux in France, and Burgos and Valladolid in Spain, carries the traveller through a picturesque and interesting country. The only stop of any importance made in France was at Bordeaux, which is situated on the Garonne River, about sixty miles from its mouth, and has a population of about two hundred thousand. The city is chiefly noted for its wines and fruits, immense quantities of both being exported annually.

From Bordeaux to the Pyrenees, the country begins to grow rugged and mountainous. On the route is Bayonne, which is three miles from the Bay of Biscay, and at the confluence of the Adour and Nive rivers, which streams divide the city into three parts. Bayonne is one of the strongest fortified cities of France. The bayonet derived its name from this place, where it was invented. Proceeding on our way towards Spain, we obtained a view of the

## By Boat and Rail. 43

"sleepless Bay of Biscay," while to the south, the Pyrenees loomed up in the distance. Crossing the Bidassoa River, which is part of the boundary between France and Spain, we entered Spain, at the town of Irun. Between this town and Madrid there are more than fifty tunnels.

Burgos, one of the principal places between Bordeaux and Madrid, was the birthplace of the celebrated Spanish hero "El Cid." Its most prominent edifice is the cathedral, one of the most magnificent in the world, in which there are said to be a miraculous image of the Saviour and a number of handsome paintings.

From Burgos to Valladolid the country is uninviting, and rugged in many places. Valladolid is a Moorish city, and at one time was the residence of the Spanish court. In this city Columbus died. It was also noted in the sixteenth century for its silver-smiths. In it, also, for a time, Cervantes, the author of *Don Quixote*, lived.

After a very tiresome ride, we reached the Spanish capital, which is surrounded by a barren and desolate country. The city has a population of half a million. The streets in the old portion are crooked and contracted; the houses are high and covered with tile. The new streets are wide and straight and handsomely adorned. Madrid is a clean city. The people are proud but polite. The men all smoke cigarettes and wear cloaks; the women are rather handsome, cover their heads with mantillas, and are given to bright colors. They have black eyes, and from the dexterity with which they turn them one would think they were afflicted with strabismus. The children are pretty, round, fat, and healthy. The beggars are numerous, and lose no time in asking for alms with one hand, while with the other they chase a certain insect over the dome of thought. Of course we had to be generous with them on account of Columbus. The Spaniard takes everything easy, is never in a hurry, and lets the other fellow wait.

Madrid contains many interesting places worth visiting. There is a fine collection of paintings in the Museo, to enumerate which would be impossible. There are Rubens, Raphaels, Murillos, Titians, and Teniers by the dozen. Connoisseurs say it is the best collection in the world, and that Spain has reason to be proud of this art gallery.

We visited the royal stables, built of marble, where there are three hundred horses and two hundred mules, mostly of Arabian and Andalusian stock. They are of the best bone, muscle, and form. There are over a hundred carriages weighed down with gold and silver, and harness to match; the woodwork of one carriage is of solid ebony. My companion obliterated all idea of the grandeur of the establishment by suggesting that it would make a first-class livery stable.

The Escurial, located twenty miles from Madrid, in a wild, mountainous country, void of beauty and dismal in the extreme, was built by Philip II. to the memory of St. Lawrence the Martyr. It is built in the shape of a gridiron, as that saint is said to have been broiled on one of those domestic articles at his martyrdom. Tradition says that he calmly told his tormentors to turn him over as he was done on that side. The king made it his residence and there ruled both Spain and America. It has sixteen courtyards, eight stairways, and eleven thousand windows, and is adorned with beautiful tapestry, carvings, and statuary. In this Pantheon are the remains of the greatest sovereigns of Spain. There are twenty-six sarcophagi of which eighteen contain the remains of kings and queens, and time will fill the rest.

## CHAPTER X.

QUITTING Madrid, we took cars for Barcelona. The first town of any historical importance through which we passed, was Alcalá de Henares, the birthplace of Cervantes, though having little else to recommend it now to the traveller. Once it was a famous seat of learning, but after the removal of the university to Madrid, it commenced to retrograde.

The next town of note was Guadalajara. It is a walled town of the mediæval times, though the walls are rapidly falling into decay. In the city, there are still a few of the picturesque Moorish houses. Here is the magnificent palace of Cardinal Mendoza, who lived like a king. It was completely sacked in 1809, when the French invaded Spain, as was also the Church of San Francisco containing the leaden coffins of the Mendozas, which were converted into bullets by the assailants.

The entire country between Madrid and this

place is barren. The next city is Zaragoza, the capital of the once renowned, but now extinct, kingdom of Aragon. It is on the Ebro River, just half-way between Madrid and Barcelona, having a population of eighty thousand. It is one of the most ancient cities of Spain and the first city of that country to profess Christianity; since that event, it has been noted for its fine collection of Christian relics. There is hardly a city in Spain which has suffered so much from war as Zaragoza. In 777, it was captured by the Moors who kept possession until 1118, when, after a siege of five years, it was retaken by the Christians; but not before nearly all of its people had been starved to death. In 1808 it suffered terribly at the hands of the French.

The siege conducted by Marshal Lannes lasted sixty-two days, and was noted for the bravery of the inhabitants, not only the men, but also the women and children, fighting for the city. Every foot of ground was contested and as the French advanced, each street, house, and even room became a battle-ground. Thirty thousand cannon-balls and sixty thousand bombs were thrown into the city. Fifty thousand citizens perished, yet, only six thousand of the number fell in fighting, the remainder becoming the victims of pestilence and famine.

There are two cathedrals in the city, one said to have been the Temple of the Goddess Diana, embellished with frescos and statuary. In it Ferdinand the Great was baptized. The other is called El Pilar, in which is a pillar where, tradition says, the Virgin descended from heaven.

The Corso is a broad street and the favorite promenade; but the other thoroughfares are narrow and gloomy. The tower of San Felipe leans, like the tower of Pisa, nine feet out of the perpendicular.

The only noteworthy place on the route between Zaragoza and Barcelona is Lerida, originally a Carthaginian city, where Cæsar defeated one of Pompey's generals. It was at one time the residence of the royal family of Aragon.

Barcelona is so old that no one seems to know when its foundation stones were laid. Hannibal's father has the credit of having rebuilt it. The country around the city is fertile and vineyards are abundant. It is the greatest manufacturing city in Spain and its handsomest town. The people are well named the "Yankees of Spain," since they are industrious and thrifty. On the land side it is surrounded by a wall and defended by a citadel. It has a good harbor, and it was here that the first attempt was made by Blasco de Garey on July 17, 1543, to apply steam as a motive power. The most ancient general bank for the deposit of cash and the issue of its own paper was established in Barcelona in 1401. There is a fine promenade, called La Rambla, which is constructed in an abandoned riverbed and planted with trees and shrubbery, resembling the Unter den Linden in Berlin. Outside of the city is the cemetery. The dead are placed in receptacles above ground, as in New Orleans, and their portraits are frequently hung above their bodies.

The people are very social and are fond of congregating at the cafés, where they drink black coffee, smoke cigarettes, and play dominos. They are fond of dress, black velvet, with red and yellow trimmings, being the favorite fabrics.

The men are generally handsome, but some of the women are perfectly beautiful; with their clean-cut features, their large flashing

## By Boat and Rail. 51

eyes, their soft black hair, their small feet and delicate hands, their Venus-like forms, and their modulated voices, one could almost imagine that there is but a step between the human and the divine.

Everything is dear, except the fare on the street-cars, which is two cents; but they do not smell "as sweet as the flowers that bloom in the spring." Fuel is expensive and little preparation is made for winter. The heat appears to be *latent*, and the cold is generally about two lengths ahead of the fire.

The houses have not an inviting appearance, and everything looks unfinished. On almost every hillside there are antiquated Moorish castles, crumbling with age and as silent as their once boisterous occupants, the tangled ivy and the sombre rooks being the only indications of life.

The people are far behind us in agricultural improvements. The oxen pull by their horns and drag a wooden plough that has but one handle. The grain is tramped out on stone floors and winnowed. There are neither fences nor hedges, and the peasantry, like those of France, live in villages. The women do their share of work, wear short petticoats and wooden shoes, and may be seen carrying heavy loads on their backs; they attend the flocks, act as flagmen at the railway stations, and labor with the men in the fields. The donkey is at home in Spain, and is seen everywhere, ever patient and overloaded; with drooping ears, he appears to be meditating over the absurdity of the Latin proverb: " Labor conquers all things."

Leaving Barcelona, with its busy marts and harbor thronged with ships from every nation, we took the train for Port Ventres, which is just over the Pyrenees in France, where we embarked for Algiers.

## CHAPTER XI.

ALGIERS is a picturesque old town, half Arab and half French, and is divided into two parts. The old town, which is the Arab portion, is a thousand years old, and is built upon the side of a hill, so steep that the ascent is made by steps. The houses rise one above another in tiers, and are annually improved by a coat of whitewash. Those of the wealthy are handsome and constructed in the Moorish style of architecture, which is light and ornamental, many of them having elaborately carved columns. There are no windows to the houses, but instead small apertures, which are protected by iron bars. The roofs are flat, and are resorted to by the occupants in the cool of the evening. The homes of the poor are mere hovels, the entrances into which are mostly below the street level.

The streets are badly paved, and so narrow, that the loaded camels cannot pass each other without friction. The balconies project so far over the street line that one can almost shake hands with his neighbor opposite. On the top of the hill is the ancient citadel, which was the castle of the old piratical Deys. When they held full sway, the castle was surmounted by an observatory, and a sentinel constantly watched for vessels sailing along the coast. The wall, which surrounds the city, is twelve feet thick and thirty feet high.

The new town was built by the French, who have been in the possession of the country for the past forty years. The streets, resembling the boulevards of Paris, are wide and made attractive by modern improvements. Algiers has no wharves, as the harbor is too shallow to allow vessels to approach close to the shore, consequently passengers, baggage, and freight are brought ashore in lighters. The porters, whose garments are not remarkable for length in either direction, will carry trunks on their backs, secured in racks, almost any distance, for a small sum.

Algiers has been frequently attacked and partially destroyed by the navies of Spain, England, Holland, and the United States.

Finally the French conquered the country and made it a colony. These repeated attacks were the result of the freebooting proclivities of the people. The French keep a *corps d'armée* of 60,000 men in Algeria, because the natives are very unreliable as to their peaceful habits. The possession of this country has cost France 150,000 soldiers and $600,000,000.

There is a greater variety of dress and language here than in any place we have visited. The Arabs still retain their white robes, and the women wear muslin over their faces, exposing nothing but their black eyes. An Arab swell, with his erect figure, standing six feet, wrapped in his fine white robe, with red morocco boots and a turban, is something to be admired. His feet are so well formed that the water will run under the instep, while, in the case of his neighbor, the negro, it will run over the foot.

The soil is very fertile, and the climate, in the winter, delightful; pomegranates, figs, dates, and oranges grow in profusion. The cereals are about the same as ours, with the exception of corn. Coral fishing is a specialty in Algiers, and is valued at $500,000 per annum. The coral is fished for by means of a wooden implement in the shape of a cross, with nets hung upon the cross-bars. These nets are dragged among the crevices of the rocks, breaking off the coral branches, which adhere to the nets.

There are some beautiful villas near the city, surrounded by gardens and luxuriant trees. Their horses, of Moorish breed, about fifteen hands high, are strong and well proportioned, and driven eight to a diligence—four abreast. With bells, crack of the whip, and shouts of the driver, they make their own right of way. Their places of worship are numerous, and represent several denominations, as the Roman Catholic cathedral, the Mohammedan mosque, the Protestant church, and the Jewish synagogue. There are some excellent hotels conducted on the French plan. A railroad runs from the city into the interior, along which eucalyptus trees have been planted to keep off the fever.

We rode in a diligence into the country as far as the Atlas Mountains. The ride in a crowded stage, filled with a job lot of Arabs, was not very pleasant. We were glad when the journey was over. It is said that brigands infest the mountains, but we were more afraid of those little robbers, of which you could cover a score with a thimble, than of the bandit with his feathers, ribbons, and little gun.

We were invited to a tiger hunt, but did not care to participate in searching for something that we did not want to find, as probably it might result in the hunter becoming the hunted.

## CHAPTER XII.

THE passage across the Mediterranean Sea from Algiers to Marseilles was rough and choppy, and the passengers were neither jovial nor loquacious.

On board was an Arab sheik, who, with a sad and landward look, was leaning over the guard of the vessel. On being asked if he liked the beautiful sea, he replied, turning up the whites of his eyes, and pointing with his long sallow finger towards the shore, that he would give a thousand piasters to hear his horse neigh on the desert. Just then the ship heaved to, and so did he. This old tub, with its round bottom, seemed to have been made on purpose to smash crockery, to break furniture, and to make things generally disagreeable. Everybody was happy when they saw the steeples and red roofs of Marseilles.

This city is said to have been founded by the Phœnicians, six centuries before the Christian era. It is the principal southern port of

## By Boat and Rail. 59

France, and has over one hundred acres of docks. The harbor can accommodate one thousand first-class vessels. At the southern entrance of the harbor is Fort St. Nicholas, and at the northern the Castle of St. Jean; out at sea are the Isles d'If, on which is the Château d'If, one of the state prisons of France, in which Mirabeau was imprisoned. It has been made more famous by the elder Dumas in his *Count of Monte Christo*. The Church of St. Victor, the Chapel of Notre Dame de la Garde with its silver image of the Virgin four feet high, the museum with its antiquities, the docks and bonded warehouses, are all worth a visit.

The harbor of Marseilles is exceedingly dirty. As there is no perceptible tide in the Mediterranean Sea, the filth that is ejected into the harbor from the city has no egress until the wind shifts to the southward. This condition of affairs has rendered the city unhealthy. The climate, except during the summer months, is delightful.

From Marseilles we journeyed to Monte Carlo, the great gambling resort of Europe since the closing of Baden-Baden in 1872. It is situated in the Principality of Monaco, the smallest and oldest monarchy in the world, and is owned by Prince Albert, who rents it to a syndicate of gamblers. The city was fortified by Louis XIV. of France, and on one of his old cannon the inscription "*Ultima ratio regum*" is still to be seen.

The drives, the gardens, the music, the picturesque lakes, the rare plants, and the Grand Casino have gained for Monte Carlo the name of an earthly paradise—a name which may fit its beauty, but not its business. The Casino, a magnificent building of cream-colored stone, is situated on the top of a promontory, one hundred and fifty feet high, overlooking the sea and surrounded by fountains, flower-beds, and tropical trees. There are free concerts every day. There are comfortable reading-rooms, and such other appointments as go to make the place agreeable.

Although it is the only place in the world where public gambling is licensed, its permanent residents are prohibited by law from taking any part therein, nor are they allowed within the Casino. Visitors must have a permit, and as they enter upon its waxed floors they are required to remove their hats. No loud talking is permitted, and everything is conducted in a decorous manner. Its tables, day and night, are crowded with people from all parts of the world, who seem anxious to throw their money away; they shower their gold on the tables, to see it raked into the coffers of the establishment by the croupiers. Women are the most persistent and the heaviest players, and lose enormous sums. Here, all day, the clink of coin, and the monotonous repetition of the croupier, *Rien ne va plus*, is heard. The Prince of Wales was there at the same time we were, and went away, like the rest who bet, several *pounds* lighter.

The only games permitted are *roulette* and *rouge-et-noir*. There are altogether ten double *roulette* tables, each twenty feet long, and four *rouge-et-noir* tables, and at some of them only gold is permitted to be played. The lowest bet that is allowed to be made at any one time is a five-franc piece, and the highest is twelve hundred francs. Ropes and pistols are sometimes in demand by those who have made unfortunate ventures at the game.

From Monte Carlo we drove over the Maritime Alps, along the Corniche road, with postilion and a spanking pair of horses with jingling bells, to Nice, for the purpose of witnessing the carnival. The road was perfect, and the scenery was enhanced by the snow-topped mountains, the bright blue sky, and trembling sea. The hills along the route were dotted with crumbling Roman towers, vineyards, and olive groves, " through whose green boughs the golden sunshine crept." These trees are planted high on the sides of the mountains, and recall to mind the dove and the olive branch. The oil is still extracted in some localities from the fruit with the old-fashioned hand-press.

The Corniche road is the finest in the world, extending from Marseilles to Genoa, a distance of over two hundred and fifty miles.

Nice formerly belonged to Sardinia, but was presented to France by Victor Emmanuel, for the military services rendered to him by Napoleon III., who helped to chase the Austrians out of Italy. The city is noted for its silk manufactories, olive oil, fine wines, and delightful climate. Although in summer Nice is excessively hot and in dry weather its streets are very dusty, yet in winter, on account of its genial climate, it is a great resort for travellers.

The carnival, which was in progress during our visit, was called the " Battle of Flowers." Wagons covered with roses were drawn along the streets, and the wheels, the horses, the harness, and the occupants were bedecked with posies. They threw bouquets to the crowd, who in turn showered them on the carriages. The air was redolent with the fragrance of the rose. Everybody appeared to be happy, for it was a day of sunshine, laughter, and flowers.

There is a marble statue in the principal street of the city, which was erected to the memory of Catherine Segurana, a poor woman who, in 1543, saved the city from capture by the Turks. Their army had planted the Crescent upon the ramparts, when she cut down the Turkish standard-bearer and rallied the flying troops.

## CHAPTER XIII.

ON the route between Nice and Pisa is the city of Genoa, reputed to be the birthplace of Columbus, though, as a matter of fact, he was born in Cogoleto, fifteen miles from Genoa, in 1447. Genoa is an attractive and historical city. It is located on a gulf, bearing the same name, at the foot of the mountains, and is a manufacturing emporium of considerable note, the principal industries being the making of furniture, velvets, silks, and hats.

The streets, as in other cities of Italy, are narrow, yet on some of them are many superb buildings. Probably it contains more palaces than any other city in the kingdom, but one gets weary gazing at so much magnificence and longs for simplicity. The style of architecture is largely *renaissante*, and the great stairways leading from the streets to the front doors glisten with marble columns. In these elegant buildings are collected many of the choicest paintings of the great masters.

## By Boat and Rail. 65

The museum has a number of documents in the handwriting of Columbus, which are now under glass, as some vandal tore his name from one of the papers. Here are many illuminated volumes, which are exceedingly well executed. It was in Genoa that for many years the leading goldsmiths had their headquarters, and a great quantity of filigree work is still manufactured there.

The women are noted for their beauty of figure, their graceful manners, and their elegant robes. The men are robust, active, and industrious.

It was in this city that Marshal Massena, one of Napoleon's generals, withstood a siege of three months against the united forces of England and Austria, with but a handful of men.

He made repeated sallies from the city, and, on one occasion, with twelve hundred men, made prisoners of four thousand Austrians. For a number of days his soldiers, prisoners, and the citizens lived upon two ounces of bread a day, made from starch, cocoa, and linseed oil. The iron-willed marshal would not surrender at discretion, as the Austrians demanded, but on the condition that he should march out of the city with flying colors, and not as prisoners of war. His terms were accepted, and, as he left the Austrian general, he remarked, "I give you notice that ere fifteen days have elapsed I shall once more be in Genoa," and he made his promise good.

From Genoa we proceeded to Pisa. The country around this city appears to be very fertile and well cultivated. Round and sleek cattle were standing in the bright streams, browsing on the low-hanging leaves, while horses were rolling and playing in the luxuriant meadows. The chief attraction of the place is the leaning tower, which is one hundred and seventy-eight feet high, fifty in diameter, and inclines thirteen feet out of the perpendicular. There is a dispute among authorities as to whether it was built in this way, or whether it was caused by settling; lawyers say it was so constructed to give it a *lien* on the land.

The river Arno divides the city into two sections, which are connected by several handsome bridges. Pisa is noted for its statuary and sculptors. The churches and public buildings are substantial and elegant in point of construction. The cathedral is one of the noblest ecclesiastical edifices in Italy, built in the form of a Latin cross, surmounted by an elliptical dome. Among its interior ornaments are magnificent bronze doors of skilful workmanship, and a grand pulpit, the work of Nicolo Pisano, the founder of the Pisan school of sculpture. This city is the birthplace of Galileo, who, one day, while in the cathredral, made the discovery of the pendulum, through the regularity with which the suspended lamps swung to and fro. Leaving Pisa we departed for Naples.

## CHAPTER XIV.

NAPLES, the beautiful, is built partly at the base and partly on the slope of two hills, facing the most renowned bay in the world. With such surroundings, it is no wonder that the Neapolitans are proud of their city, and say "See Naples and die"; but we would rather see the Brandywine Hills and live. Naples has a population of half a million; the people are industrious, sober, and genial, and one hears more laughter than blasphemy. The workmen are strong, and the wages are much lower than in this country, and living is cheap. Fruit and vegetables are abundant, and, in the evenings, herds of goats, with tinkling bells are driven through the streets, to be milked at the doors of the customers.

The city, so the people say, is so ancient, that the time of its commencement is unknown. Some of the houses verify the statement. Many of them are a hundred feet high, with walls eight feet thick. The streets are narrow and crowded to excess. In the evening the Riviera di Chiaja, that splendid and fashionable thoroughfare, is thronged with pedestrians and stylish equipages, but the most remarkable vehicle in Naples is the *coricolo*, which is a public conveyance drawn by one horse, and seems to have a capacity far beyond its size. It is not limited to numbers, as twenty or thirty persons often ride in or on it; every available space, except the wheels is occupied, and a net is swung beneath, in which the children are stowed.

There are over a hundred churches of all styles of architecture, a dozen well conducted hospitals, two dozen good hotels, and scores of artistic fountains, which make the city attractive. There is a good supply of water brought from Serino, about thirty miles distant.

The donkey, the horse, and the cow are hitched together, while the dogs and the women do their share of work. Soldiers are numerous, assuming an air of satisfaction, as they do not expect an enemy to come, and have none to pursue.

In some quarters of the city the inhabitants are prolific in rags, dirt, and children; if they had a day fixed for a grand wash, it would be a benefit both to themselves and to the soil. The land is composed of volcanic ashes, mixed with decomposed vegetation. There is a stone called *piperino*, which is not as heavy as marble, used in the manufacture of columns for buildings. The streets are paved with blocks of lava, which are hard and even. The principal church is the cathedral, which is located upon the ancient site of the Temple of Apollo. In it is the chief entrance to the catacombs.

The royal palace is decorated with artistic frescos by native artists. The museum contains the royal library of nearly two hundred thousand volumes, and an unrivalled collection of gems, mosaics, bronzes, and vases, taken from the ruins of Pompeii and Herculaneum.

Naples, in 1885, suffered terribly from the cholera, as many as fifteen hundred people dying in a single day; now it is considered healthy. The hotels are excellent, but they charge extra for light, soap, and attendance, and the traveller is expected to pay all hands when he takes his departure.

There are entire streets in Naples devoted to stores, in which nothing but the images of

## By Boat and Rail.   71

saints and *madonnas* are sold. These images are of the most brilliant colors. Thousands of them are exported to the United States and South America; in fact, wherever the Italian goes, the saints and *madonnas* follow.

The Neapolitans have great veneration for their dead. On All-Souls-Day it is their custom to visit the cemeteries and decorate the graves of their relatives. For the performance of this they make a kind of holiday, and go on their mission in a reverential manner; but, this duty being performed, they enter the inns, and with bacchanal song and laughter soon forget their dead. The people have also a very curious custom of exhuming the body two years after interment, and having the bones washed and then reburied. Some mothers even encase the bones of their little ones in a small casket, and wear them around their necks.

Mount Vesuvius is on the opposite side of the Bay of Naples. There is an excellent carriage road to the base of the cone, from which a cable road runs nearly to the top. Here is a restaurant, where you can procure a good lunch and the celebrated wine, " Lacryma

Christi," which is made from the vineyards planted along its abrupt sides.

After reaching the terminus, we climbed through ashes and lava to the crater, assisted by the guide, who pulled us up by placing a band around our shoulders. We were near enough to light paper and burn our shoes. The volcano was at the time emitting smoke, fire, and stones. We were almost overcome by the fumes of sulphur, and were slightly agitated by the terrific rumbling, so we were perfectly satisfied to retrace our steps and take the cars for safer quarters. We visited Pompeii, which is at the base of the mountain. The city was destroyed in the year 79 A.D. In 1748, the buried town was discovered while a vineyard was being planted. Since that date, frequent excavations have been made, and now about one quarter of it has been exposed. The streets were paved with lava, where the tracks of wheels can still be seen; on each side were footpaths, under which were channels, closed by iron bars, intended to carry away the waters; about twenty-five streets have been reopened, the widest being thirty feet. The houses were two stories high, without chimneys, containing

# By Boat and Rail. 73

a vestibule, a court, in the centre of which was a flower garden, with basins and fountains and baths.

The worn marble at the fountains, of which there is one in every street, still show their excessive use. They had forums, theatres, and private residences, elaborately decorated with mosaics and columns. Some of the stores were large and handsome. From the surroundings, it seemed that the people must have lived luxuriantly.

The skeletons of many were exhumed, lying in the position in which they fell, suffocated by the heat and ashes. Soldiers were found standing at their posts; animals, exhibiting the last agonies of death; people, apparently in flight, clutching treasures in their hands. Surgical instruments, similar to those of the present day, as well as exquisite statuary in marble, bronze, and brass, were observed.

In one house we visited was an artist's studio, in which there was a marble slab, half cut. Several unfinished figures and the tools used by the artist were lying near by. Everything had the appearance of the occupant having left the room in great haste. Among the every-day necessities were terra-cotta pipes for heating purposes, lead pipes with water stops, and mills for grinding grain. The shops of wine-merchants and money-changers made one think that he was in a modern instead of an ancient city.

The secret passage by which the priests entered the statue of Isis, to make her propound the oracles, was one of the most interesting discoveries. The temple contained ten altars, on which were burned the bodies of animals; their bones and ashes were still lying around the altars.

We saw the house of Sallust, which was identified by an inscription over the door. Pompeii, with its salubrious climate and sunny hills, the bright sea, the mountain, and the plain, must have been an earthly paradise.

We also visited Herculaneum, which suffered with its sister city. Its locality was discovered in 1706, when a well was being sunk. It also must have been an attractive place. The streets were wide and straight, the buildings even finer than those of Pompeii. One of the theatres, generously ornamented with bronzes and marble statuary, was capacious enough to seat eight thousand persons.

## By Boat and Rail.    75

Before our departure from Naples we visited the tomb of Virgil, whose enchanting verses will last as long as the hills and valleys of which he sang so sweetly. We also saw the house in which, at one time, Nero resided.

On the opposite side of the bay from Naples is the ancient city of Sorrento, which was the birthplace of the poet Tasso. His house is still standing, having been built upon a rock.

" Beside Sorrento's sounding beach, on which her murm'ring seas
   Their blue waves roll 'mid foam and spray beneath the orange trees."

There are still left some of the old ruins, such as those of the temples of Ceres and of the Sirens. In the days of the greatness of Rome, as now, this place was celebrated for the purity of its air and the charm of its scenery. The wines which came from the vineyards of Sorrento were held in high repute.

## CHAPTER XV.

OUR next objective point was Rome,— the Eternal City,—and headquarters of the Roman Catholic Church. Although the Pope has been deprived of his temporal power, and rules over no territory, yet he is a very important personage, and has a larger number of subjects than any other ruler.

While in Rome the guides promised to show us things that had been, and even things that were not. They were as flippant about the palaces of the Cæsars as if they had assisted in the building, and one might suppose, from their style of language and the attitudes which they assumed, that they had been orators in the Forum, gladiators in the Colosseum, and had even knocked about with Septimius Servius.

We wandered through the grand palaces, shining with gold and silver, visited the churches built over the remains of heathen temples, admired the triumphal arches and the gigantic baths, and stood beside solid aqueducts which

# By Boat and Rail. 77

seemed as imperishable as their history. We visited the Tarpeian Rock and the tombs of the Scipios; we heard the owls hoot in the aisles of the Colosseum, and watched the moonlight upon the walls; we scared the rooks from the broken baths of Caracalla, and saw lizards basking in the sun at the Egerian fountain. We saw cows in the Forum with its acres of ruins, and heard the donkey bray where Cicero harangued the people.

In Rome objects of general curiosity and special faith abound. The Cathedral of St. Peter—the largest church in the world—is in the form of a Latin cross, and is surmounted by three domes, which on Easter and other great festal days of the Church are illuminated by five thousand lights. The height of the central dome from the floor to the top of the cross is 435 feet, and its diameter is 196 feet; the dome of this church is, therefore, fifty feet wider and sixty-four feet higher than St. Paul's in London. The length of the church is 613 feet, and across the transepts 450 feet. The vaulted dome is ornamented with gilded decorations; the pavement is of marble inlaid in designs. The high altar, over the grave of St.

Peter, has a rich canopy, supported by four beautiful spiral bronze columns. Here high mass is only celebrated by the Pope. The cupola is embellished with figures in mosaics; the doors of the cathedral are all of bronze, and are in bas-relief of the most exquisite workmanship. There is a bronze statue of St. Peter, who is represented as sitting in a chair, and as the " faithful " pass they kneel and kiss his toe, which has become worn thin by this mark of adoration. There are a number of statues in the cathedral the work of Michael Angelo, Thorwaldsen, Canova, and others.

The Vatican, which is the residence of the Pope, contains a great number of celebrated paintings and manuscripts. In the Sistine Chapel there are also many grand paintings. Among the most notable in the Sistine Chapel are *The Last Judgment* and *Creation of the World*, by Michael Angelo. In the Vatican are *The Transfiguration* and *The Adoration of the Magi*, by Raphael; also three Murellos, which are as beautiful and true as paintings can be made.

In the Church of St. John Lateran, founded by Constantine, the guide showed us, what is

## By Boat and Rail. 79

said to be a part of the table used at the Last Supper, also the holy staircase formed of twenty-eight marble steps, formerly in the house of Pilate, which had been brought to Rome. This stair is called holy from having been sanctified by the blood of Christ, who ascended and descended it at the period of his trial. They are covered with boards to prevent them from being worn away by the thousands of the faithful who ascend them upon their knees, as a penance for their sins. At another place is shown the prison of St. Peter; the well from which he drank, which is still full of water; the chains with which he was bound, and the spot where he was crucified head downward. The Pantheon, that magnificent temple erected by Agrippa, in the centre of the Campus Martius, is now the only building of ancient Rome which remains entire.

The Church of the Capuchins, near the Barberini Palace, contains the famous painting of *St. Michael the Archangel*, by Guido. The church is both the home and the sepulchre of the Capuchin friars, who are very strict in their devotions and habits. They bury their members in the vaults of the church, which, being very limited, cause them to adopt a peculiar custom, which is, to exhume the bones of those who have been buried for some time to make place for others who have recently died. They pile the dry skulls in tiers, one above another, and make rosettes and other designs of the smaller bones. Some of the more prominent of the order have had their bones kept intact, and are dressed in cowl and cassock. An old friar, who was showing us through the crypt, remarked in a jocular manner: "Some day my bones will decorate this room."

While in Rome we saw the Pope officiating as high priest and washing the feet of pilgrims. We also met the King and Queen driving out. They saluted every one, and my companion, Dr. R. J. Baily, remarked: "They seem to be the only speaking acquaintances that we have in this country." We visited a theatre over which there was no roof, and the play was *Christopher Columbus Discovering America;* all the Indians wore long beards, which struck us as ludicrous.

We became weary looking at the paintings, statuary, ruins, palaces, and churches of this great city. It is easy to see that the present

## By Boat and Rail. 81

Romans are not related to the ancient inhabitants. None of the present race have ever sculptured *The Dying Gladiator* nor painted *The Transfiguration*, nor raised the columns of the Colosseum; they are better at raising prices.

Recently the sewerage of the city has undergone some radical changes, and Rome has been made one of the healthiest cities in Europe. The streets are kept clean, and most excellent water from the mountains has been introduced. There is now a project to construct a canal from the city to the sea; if built, it will be about twelve miles long. The cost is estimated at twenty million dollars. Rome is a cosmopolitan city, and is full of priests, beggars, and sight-seers. In the country the fashion never changes; the peasants have much the same style of dress that they had in the days of Horace, and the changes of the modes do not trouble them any more than politics and other luxuries. In the summer they come down from the mountains to gather the crops, driving long-horned cream-colored oxen, which draw huge loads over the Appian Way. In the time of the vintage, which is the happiest and merriest of the year, when the gentle wind plays among the tangled vines, and the sparkling sunshine mellows the purple of the pendant clusters, the peasants make the vine-clad hills of Albano and Palestrina ring with Vendemmian song in anticipation of the blushing harvest:

> " 'T is enough to make
> The sad man merry, the benevolent one
> Melt into tears, so general is the joy."

In every direction from Rome there are to be seen the remains of ancient cities,—Tivoli, Frascati, the villa of Adriana, and Veii. Of the last mentioned city, Propertius said : " Now within the walls the horn of the herdsman sounds slowly, and they reap the fields among your bones."

The Italians have some very curious customs, which have been preserved and handed down from generation to generation. Their dances are lively and noisy, being generally performed in the open air, accompanied with music and song. The *canta-storia*, or story-singer, is one who tells a romance in rhyme. This custom is one of the most ancient. In some sections the people will not eat a tame goose, because the ancient Romans made the goose a sacred bird, as by their cackling they gave notice of the approach of the Gauls, and thereby saved the city.

All over Italy are found macaroni manufactories, as this delicacy is a favorite dish with all classes, and, to a great extent, the substitute for bread; it is sold everywhere, in the shops and upon the streets; it is macaroni and olives in the palaces and cottages, year in and year out. Chestnuts are an important crop; they make bread and other articles of diet from them, and the failure of this crop is a serious one.

## CHAPTER XVI.

FLORENCE, one of the most pleasantly located cities of Europe, lies among the mountains and forests of Tuscany, and is divided by the " golden Arno," which is crossed by several bridges. One, the Ponto della Santa Trinita, is of marble, remarkable for its elegance and lightness, and is adorned with statues.

Florence has had associated with its history the names of more illustrious men than any other city. Lorenzo de Medici, Macchiavelli, and Amerigo Vespucci were born here. It was the home of the great poet Dante, whose tomb, with those of Michael Angelo, Galileo, and Villanis, is in the Church of Santa Croce.

The proudest boast of Florence is the grand gallery in the Uffizi Palace, containing specimens of painting and statuary by the greatest masters. In statuary may be specified the *Venus de Medici*, and the group of *Niobe and Her Children;* and in painting, works by Michael Angelo, Raphael, Titian, Guido, and numerous others. In the Pitti Palace is Raphael's *Madonna della Seggiola*, the most beautiful picture extant. In order to copy this picture, application must be made five years beforehand, so many desire to reproduce it. Some of the rooms were laid in mosaic, and the walls covered with admirably executed tapestries.

The Laurentian Library contains upwards of nine thousand ancient manuscripts, equalled in importance by no collection, except that of the Vatican.

The Duomo, which is the famous cathedral, has the largest dome in the world. The people are chiefly engaged in marble-cutting, wood-carving, cabinet-making, working in mosaics, gold-beating, and silver-smithing. There are also porcelain and majolica factories.

Florence is a clean city. The climate is mild, the attractions numerous, the surroundings charming, the inhabitants social, and living is cheap.

Bologna is one of the great educational centres of Europe. Its university is as venerable as any in the world. The Botanical Gardens contain a great number of rare and beautiful plants. These gardens were established by the famous anatomist and botanist, Aldrovandi, who is said to have died in one of the hospitals that he founded.

This city has the reputation of having produced more popes and cardinals than any other. It was the birthplace of the painters Guido, Albano, and Barbiere; the astronomer, Marsigli; the naturalist, Galvani, and other celebrities. It is from this city that the celebrated Bologna sausages obtain their name. The demand for this article was evidently greater than the supply, as was indicated by the brevity of the caudal appendages of some of the animals.

On our way to Venice we stopped at Mantua. The country is rather flat; and we observed peasants cutting clover, the heads of which are of a bright crimson. The stalks grow taller and the heads much longer than the clover in this country.

Our entrance into Mantua was made with some mental enthusiasm, no doubt, on account of its association with the name of Virgil. It is a walled town on the river Po, from which stream its moats can be rapidly filled; these, now useless modes of defence, were first constructed around it by the Emperor Charlemagne.

In our travels through Italy, the songsters we heard were the skylark, the nightingale, the thrush, the linnet, and the cuckoo, that lays her eggs in other birds' nests, and like

"The whippoorwill, her name her only song."

# CHAPTER XVII.

VENICE, aquatic Venice, built on piles and occupying seventy islands, is separated by numerous canals, which are crossed by three hundred and fifty bridges; thus the streets are canals, whose hacks are boats. The footways are from ten to fifteen feet wide, and the only wheeled vehicle that can be used is the wheelbarrow. The palaces resemble a fleet, floating upon the waters, from the windows of which one could fish, and bathe from the front door.

This, then, is blue-skied Venice, of which the poets have written so much, with her sweet language and bitter smells. The water of the Grand Canal is of a bright green color, making a rich contrast with the deep blue of the sky and the brilliant hue of the marble houses. The gondolas move through the waterways swiftly and almost silently. At night, they carry lanterns, and then occasionally can be heard the sound of the guitar and the voice of

*By Boat and Rail.* 89

singers, as they glide along through the liquid streets.

The palaces are famous, and the workmanship upon some of the doors is of the most exquisite style. The palace of the Doges recalls all that was glorious and cruel in Venetian history. It is filled with allegorical frescos and rich paintings by Titian, Veronese, and others. Of the seventy-two Doges, who have ruled over Venice, the portraits of seventy-one hang upon the walls; the one whose portrait was not placed there was Marino Falieri, who was beheaded for the crime of endeavoring to overthrow the Republic, and he is represented by a black space. The palace is connected with the prison, which has two stories of dark cells below the water-level, by the Bridge of Sighs, which has been made so famous by Lord Byron in his *Childe Harold.*

The Rialto is still, as it was in the days of Shylock, the place of news. The island of Rialto at the bend of the Grand Canal is the largest piece of ground in the city. On it was built the first house in Venice.

St. Mark is the great historical church, being built in the form of a Greek cross, and having a central dome with four smaller ones, all being surmounted by crosses. It has been made the receptacle of historical paintings. This cathedral is situated on the Piazza di San Marco, and every day, at noon, thousands of pigeons are fed at the expense of the government; so tame have they become, that they will feed from the hand. These pigeons are protected by law; just as the turkey-buzzard is in some of our states, though not for the same purpose.

In front of the Piazzetta, which opens upon the sea, stand two magnificent granite obelisks, on one of which is a statue of St. Theodore, and on the other, the winged Lion of St. Mark, which was the coat-of-arms of the Venetian Republic. Over the doorway of St. Mark are four celebrated bronze horses, which were brought to Venice from Constantinople in 1205; tradition says that they are very ancient, and were found in Alexandria by Cæsar Augustus, when he conquered Antony, and by him were taken to Rome. When Constantine became Emperor, and moved his capital to Constantinople, he took these horses with him. During the reign of Napoleon I. they were

## By Boat and Rail. 91

removed from Venice to Paris, but after his abdication they were restored to the Venetians. They are the only horses they have and are much prized. Though great travellers and exceedingly old, they are still sound and full of *metal.*

Many of the elegant palaces have been converted into furniture and bead bazaars. The manufacture of peculiar and beautiful beads is one of the principal industries of Venice; on the island of Murano there are thousands of artists employed entirely in this branch of trade. The glass is first drawn into long tubes made in a variety of colors, then the colored tubes are twisted together, thereby blending all into every shade of the rainbow; after which they are cut into little pieces and stirred upon hot pans, until the sharp edges are rendered smooth and the bead round. Hundreds of children are employed stringing them. Any one, who has once visited Venice and witnessed the manufacture of these beads, would recognize them in any part of the world. It is said that tons of them are shipped every year into Africa for traffic.

Recently there has been built a breakwater,

which extends two miles into the sea. This has greatly improved the facilities for shipping.

The women are engaged in lace-making and the manufacture of artificial flowers, and the men in wood-carving and the making of superb glassware.

## CHAPTER XVIII.

QUITTING Venice and her palaces, and crossing the blue Adriatic, we reached Trieste, the chief seaport of the Austrian Empire, and a thoroughly cosmopolitan city. The fish-market is fine. The epicurean fish is the tunny, which frequently measures six feet in length and weighs from five hundred to one thousand pounds. In appearance it somewhat resembles a gigantic mackerel, and has a fine flavor. The catching of these fish forms one of the chief occupations of the people.

While strolling around the old town we lost our way and were unable to extricate ourselves from the crooked streets. Appeals were made to several natives as to the location of the Vienna railroad station, but they were unable to understand, because they called Vienna " Wien." Finally, by imitating the noise of a locomotive, they took in the situation and conducted us to the station.

The custom-house officers and police of Austria are very diligent, one going through your baggage, while the other examines your passport. Probably Vienna is the gayest capital of Europe, its only rival being Paris, and is equal to the French capital in the opportunities afforded for amusement and society. Its streets, arched with lime and horse-chestnut trees, were wide and handsome, crowded with monuments and statuary of celebrated Austrians, and the gardens were delicious with the bloom of exotic flowers. An agricultural exhibition was in progress, crowded with all kinds of domestic animals, from bantams to Percheron horses. The spectators, under the shade of the wide-spreading trees, quaffed kegs of beer and destroyed large quantities of bretzels and mal-odorous cheese, to show that they relished the occasion and honored the national beverage. There are both electrical and horse railroads, and the fare is but four cents.

Vienna is the residence of the imperial family. The royal jewel office and museum are filled with curiosities. Here is the coronation regalia of Charlemagne, which was taken from his tomb at Aix-la-Chapelle, and which has been used at all the coronations of the emperors of the Holy Roman Empire and Austria. There are also on exhibition a tooth which is said to have belonged to St. John the Baptist, a portion of the coat of St. John the Divine, and a piece of the table-cloth used at the Last Supper; all of which statements you are at liberty to believe if you so desire. There are also the crown, sceptre, and robes which were worn by Napoleon I. when he was crowned, at Milan, as King of Lombardy; the cradle of the King of Rome, the son of Napoleon; the richly jewelled sword of Tamerlane, with its blade of finest steel; and the battle-axe of Montezuma, sent from Mexico by the ill-fated Emperor Maximilian.

Two miles from the city is the Schönbrunn, the summer residence of the Emperor; the palace is richly furnished, and was occupied by Napoleon I. when he was in possession of the Austrian capital. While in this palace he had two doors at the entrance of his bed-chamber, and between them a guard stood who filled up the entire space; thus access could not be gained to the Emperor's sleeping apartments while the guard was on duty. This palace was also the home of his son, the King of Rome, who, after the abdication, was taken by his Austrian mother from France back to her own country, and given the title of the Duke de Reichstadt. The young Prince died in this palace in 1832. The room is unchanged, and the bed upon which he died is still in the same position. He was always guarded by his grandfather, the Emperor Francis I., for fear that the French would kidnap him and make him Emperor of France.

In the Capuchin church, which is the burial-place of Austrian royalty, there are seventy metal caskets, containing the remains of every emperor since the days of Matthias, who died in 1619; but the most sought for is that of the young Napoleon.

## CHAPTER XIX.

THE journey from Vienna to Berlin is delightful, the country being dotted with small towns, extensive forests, well cultivated farms, and hills terraced with vineyards and covered with windmills. We made a short stop at Prague, a city of universities and revolutions. It was here that the Hussites, under Ziska, fought for the Reformation, and it was from the windows of the Hradschin, the palace of the Bohemian kings, that the Protestants threw Martinitz and Slawata, two unpopular members of the imperial government. It was this act that initiated the Thirty Years' War. Here, in 1348, the first free university in Germany was planted by the Emperor Charles IV., after whom it was named. At the head of this school were John Huss and Jerome of Prague, who opposed the Roman Catholics.

From Prague we proceeded to Dresden, which is located on the Elbe. This river divides the city into two parts, across which is a bridge. This bridge was built with the money procured from the sale of indulgences, granted by the Pope to the people who wished to eat butter and meat during Lent. One of the piers of this bridge was blown up by Marshal Davoust on his retreat from the city.

The museum is filled with war implements: the iron-shod flails, with which the Hussites fought the Catholics; the battle-axes, spears, and armors which were used before the introduction of gunpowder; the boots which were worn by Napoleon at the battle of Dresden, and a pair of his satin slippers used at his coronation; also the cocked hat of Peter the Great. In the royal palace is the "Green Vault," which is a mine of jewels, richer far than those of Arabian tales.

From Dresden we went to Berlin, which boasts of eight thousand acres of public parks, a university of three thousand students, and an enormous library, always open. The art gallaries are hung with pictures by native artists.

Its streets are regular and exceedingly clean, the most noticeable being the Unter den Linden, which has a double row of trees. This makes a delightful promenade, and was the

## By Boat and Rail. 99

favorite drive of the late Emperor Wilhelm I. Many of the squares are named after the great princes of Brandenburg and kings of Prussia. The police are polite and vigilant, and the landlords and hackmen have fixed prices.

Every boy in Berlin can read, as the government compels him to go to school; and, at some time in his life, every man is a soldier. The Protestant religion prevails, and the tendency of the people is towards a free government. They speak the best German, have the fewest poor, and the fairest laws of any people on the continent. The women are pretty, healthy, and strong, and appear to be frugal, nevertheless they are all *waist*.

The city owns a number of public baths, which are open from June to September. The population is about a million and a half, and during the year about half a million people visit the city. All the meat used is subject to an inquisitorial examination by inspectors, and that which does not come up to the standard is seized and burned.

The present Emperor seems to be able and competent, and in case of a dispute with other nations no doubt he would be able to hold his own with pen or sword.

## CHAPTER XX.

AFTER enjoying the sights of the capital of Germany, we again started for the south of Europe, passing through Leipsic, one of the university cities of Germany, its college being second in age to that of Prague. This city is also noted for its fairs, three being held annually, each lasting nearly a month. Leipsic is a famous book mart; there is hardly a volume published that does not at some time find its way into the city.

The old house called "Auerbach's Cellar," near the market, has the reputation of having been the haunt of the celebrated Dr. Faustus, and in the same cellar Goethe laid the scene of his famous story of Faust and Mephistopheles.

On the plains surrounding Leipsic, the great battle between Napoleon with 160,000 men and the allies under the Emperors of Russia and Austria with 240,000, was fought. The contest lasted three days, and is known as "The Battle of Nations" Here Prince

Poinatowiski, the Polish prince, and one of Napoleon's marshals, lost his life in the river Elster, when, with a handful of brave countrymen, he covered the retreat of the French army.

Our route took us through Nuremberg, Ratisbon, Munich, and Verona, to Milan.

Nuremberg has about eighty thousand inhabitants, who reside in houses of antique style of architecture, with gabled roofs and stone balconies. It has a double line of fortified walls guarded by seventy towers.

Ratisbon has a population of thirty thousand. Its chief places of interest are the Rathhaus and its old cathedral. In the former are located the dungeons and chamber of torture. In the latter are still shown the implements of torture, such as the rack, the chair of spikes, the ropes and pulleys, and the wooden horse with back as sharp as a razor.

Milan, one of the principal cities of Italy, with a population of over two hundred thousand, is situated in the centre of the great plains of Lombardy. The city is circular, and is surrounded by a wall which has ten gates. Here is the cathedral, one of the most noted churches in Europe, having a dome three hundred and thirty-five feet high. In this edifice, in 1805, Napoleon was crowned King of Italy. He created the city, the capital of the new kingdom. Close to the cathedral is the imperial palace, which was the residence of Napoleon whenever he visited Milan.

From here we went to Turin, the old capital of Piedmont, which has about the same number of inhabitants as Milan. The people are industrious, and in comfortable circumstances, but few beggars being among them. Leaving Turin, we continued our journey towards Geneva, which carried us through the Mount Cenis tunnel, one of the greatest pieces of engineering skill that has ever been accomplished. The tunnel is nearly eight miles long, and 9,700 feet above sea-level. The work was commenced January 25, 1863, and completed December 31, 1870. The work was carried on from both the French and the Italian sides of the Alps, and, on the last day, the two engineering forces met exactly half-way through the mountain.

On a subsequent visit to Europe we passed from Italy into Switzerland through the Mount

St. Gothard tunnel, which is over nine miles long, and completed in 1881. After passing into France, you enter the highly cultivated department of Savoy. The route takes the traveller through the ancient town of Chambery, which is noted for its manufacture of silk gauze. A ride of less than two hours lands you in Geneva, which is the principal and best known city of Switzerland.

## CHAPTER XXI.

GENEVA is situated at the foot of Lake Geneva, which is fifty-three miles long, eight, wide, and, in some places, 1,150 feet deep. The lake is fed by the Rhone, and a large number of little streams, which flow into it from the snow-clad mountains. The country around Geneva indicates prosperity, as all the farms are neat and clean.

The city is an ancient one, having a population of fifty thousand, and lies on each side of the Rhone. A number of terraced walks are laid out on the old wall, which once defended the city. The Cathedral of St. Pierre is situated in the most elevated part of the city. Geneva was the first town of Europe to accept the doctrines of the Reformation. Its university was founded by John Calvin, who lived and died here. It was the native place of the celebrated Jean Jacques Rousseau, to whose memory a statue was erected in one of the public squares.

There are no beggars on the streets of Geneva. They are a forbidden luxury. The Genevese say that there is no necessity for these mendicants, as there is always an abundance of work. The chief industries are the manufacture of watches, musical boxes, jewelry, and curios. Over seven thousand people get their living by these branches of industry, and every year over a hundred thousand watches and hundreds of thousands of musical instruments are made.

The climate is variable, but the air is pure. In and around Geneva there are many places of interest, the lake furnishing the greater portion. At its upper end is the castle of Chillon, which is out in the lake on a barren rock. It was built for a prison, and in it was confined Bonnivard, for trying to free Geneva from the yoke of Amadeus IV., Duke of Savoy. He was chained in one of the dungeons for six years. Lord Byron has immortalized the castle by his famous poem, *The Prisoner of Chillon.*

Vevay and Lausanne, two towns on the north side of the lake, are favorite resorts. In the latter city John Kemble, the celebrated actor, lived for several years after his retirement from the stage. Here also lived Gibbon, the historian, while he wrote the *Decline and Fall of the Roman Empire*. In the cathedral the visitor is shown a piece of the true Cross, some of the Virgin's hair, and a rib of Mary Magdalene.

## CHAPTER XXII.

TO reach Mt. Blanc from Geneva, we took a diligence in the morning and drove through a lovely country to the village of Chamouni, which is in a valley of the same name. The night was spent at one of the excellent inns, and the next morning the ascent was commenced.

Our party consisted of six, all well mounted upon mules. The route was via the Mer-de-Glace. This wonderful sea of ice is broken, here and there, by fissures, in whose unknown depths can be heard the gurgling of the waters. It is perfectly clear, but, on account of its density and thickness, has a dark-blue appearance. The Montanvert is one of the resting points, from which is obtained a good view of the Mer. The next rest is at the Jardin, which is a small, earth-covered rock, seemingly out of place in this wilderness of ice. The trip up the mountain is very exciting, requiring a sharp lookout on the part of the traveller, lest he may disappear down some chasm. The trip, however, pays. The downward journey is a more rapid one, and sometimes against the will of the individual, and it is then that lives are mostly lost, by missing a foothold. Away goes the unfortunate one down the declivities, as if he were on a toboggan slide!

The next day we returned to Geneva. From here we went to Berne. The country was bright with green fields, and the grass looked like a thick velvet carpet, on which were feeding large herds of cattle. The farms were small but well cared for, and the dairies presented a very inviting appearance.

Berne, having a population of about forty thousand, is one of the finest cities of Europe. Its name is simply the German for our English word "Bear." Tradition says that Berthold V., a Swiss duke, killed a bear on the site of the present city, and, in commemoration of the event, commenced building this town. It is the capital of the Swiss Confederation. Streams of water flow through its streets, as in Salt Lake City; the water is clear and limpid from the Bernese Alps, which can be seen in the distance.

Among the curious sights of the city are the old-fashioned watch-towers and the clock-tower; the latter is located in the centre of the town, and, just as the hour is struck, a wooden rooster comes out of a door, crows twice, and flaps its wings; then a puppet appears, with a hammer in its hand, and strikes the hour upon a bell; after this a procession of bears comes out and passes before the figure of Duke Berthold, who gives a yawn for each hour, lowers his sceptre, and the figures disappear until the next hour comes around.

There is also a bear-pit, in which a number of these animals are confined to keep up the tradition. Into the pit an Englishman once fell; and the keepers were much put out, as it was not the hour for feeding the animals.

From Berne we turned our faces towards France by way of Basel. It is a city of about fifty thousand people, and is situated on the Rhine, close to the famous Black Forest. The chief industry is the manufacture of ribbons. From Basel we crossed into France and proceeded to Paris, through one of the most fertile sections of country that can be found anywhere on the continent.

## CHAPTER XXIII.

AFTER a brief stay in the gay capital of France we proceeded to Calais, and crossed the channel to Dover. From here we returned to London, pleased once more to hear our native language spoken.

From London we took the train for Chester, passing through Rugby, noted as an educational centre, and as the place where Thomas Hughes, the author, laid the scene of his celebrated book, *Tom Brown's School Days*. As we steamed along, the ivy-covered church and the famous school-house were visible. The next town of importance was one that recalled to memory Chester County—Birmingham, one of the famous manufacturing cities of England. It has a population of about 300,000, and is built upon the banks of the river Rea. It is famous for its make of hardware, swords, and fire-arms. It was here that the discovery of electroplating was made. With regard to health, it is one of the healthiest cities in the kingdom. The cause of the low death-rate has been attributed to the large quantity of vitriol that is used in the factories.

A ride of sixty miles carried us to Chester, after which, Chester, Delaware County, and West Chester were named. This is one of the oldest cities in England. It is situated on the river Dee, and was the head-quarters of the Twelfth Legion of the Roman army, when it came to England in the year 60 A.D. It has been called Neomagus, after Magus, a grandson of Japhet, who, legend says, founded it about two hundred years after the Flood; next it was called Cærlleon, in honor of the giant Leon Vaur; then Cærleil, after a British king. After the Romans took possession, they named it Cær-legion, but the Latin historians called it Castra, which means a camp. The name went through the following evolutions, Deunana, Deva, Devana, Civitas, Legan Chester, Lege Chester, West Chester, and finally Chester. It was a walled city, and portions of the wall are still preserved, but instead of a means of defence it is used as a promenade, being nearly two miles in length. The wall was pierced by four gates. There is an excellent museum, in which have been collected from the excavations, Roman coins, pottery, altars, works of art, columns, tesselated pavements, monuments, and tablets bearing Roman inscriptions.

The cathedral, which is of Gothic architecture, is very imposing and elaborately embellished. There are a number of other churches, all of which are interesting. A Friends' meeting-house, is of the same plain and unassuming appearance that distinguishes those in our own country.

In 1643, Chester underwent a siege of two years, the result of a conflict between the king and the people, in which the former came off victorious. The castle, in which the Earls of Chester lived, was built during the reign of William the Conqueror, in 1060, but the original edifice has been supplanted by a more modern building, although upon the same site. About three miles from Chester is Eaton Hall, the residence of the Marquis of Westminster, who is one of the richest men in England.

From Chester we proceeded to Liverpool, where we took a steamer for Belfast, passing the Isle of Man, noted for its tailless cats. This island is about as large as Delaware County,

Pennsylvania. The people speak the Celtic language, and, along the coast, are chiefly engaged in the herring and cod fisheries; in the interior there are good grazing lands.

Belfast has a world-wide reputation as being the city where the best Irish linen is manufactured—in fact, the finest in the world. In one of the mills, where over two thousand hands are employed, they turn out enough linen to shirt the whole country. Goods are cheap and so is labor. Women work in the mills for a shilling a day. In Belfast, as in every town of importance in Ireland, the English soldier is stationed; which has much the same effect upon Irishmen that a red flag has upon a bull. The British vigilance has a tendency to keep them in a continual state of excitement. In the province of Ulster, County Antrim, north of Belfast, a Celtic colony from Scotland settled, who became the progenitors of the Scotch-Irish.

Ireland is a lovely country of lakes and undulating pastures. The atmosphere is moist and the temperature even. Its chief agricultural products are potatoes, barley, flax, grass, and oats.

One fourth of the entire acreage of the

country is under cultivation. It is free from snakes and toads, and is filled with legends, shamrock, and blackthorn. The people are honest and free-hearted. They worship their heroes, love their whiskey, are loyal to the Pope, and hate their English masters.

Dublin, the capital, is the residence of the Lord-Lieutenant, who is always an Englishman. Originally it was called "Bally-athcliath," which means the "Ford of the Hurdles," but more recently the name was changed to Dubh-linn, or "Black Pool." It is one of the chief cities in the British Empire. The river Liffey divides it, and along the water front are great embankments, constructed of granite, and lined with magnificent quays.

Dublin Castle is the residence of the Lord-Lieutenant. It is an interesting edifice, as in its construction every style of architecture seems to have been combined. The council-chamber contains the portraits of all the Lord-Lieutenants. In St. Patrick's Hall, another room in the Castle, which is over eighty feet long, forty, wide, and thirty-eight, high, the ceiling is painted in three parts. In the centre is a circular representation of George III. supporting Liberty and Justice; the second fresco is the conversion of the Irish by St. Patrick, and the third is that of the submission of the Irish chiefs to Henry II. In another part of the castle are the busts of St. Peter, the Virgin, St. Patrick, Brian Boru, Dean Swift, and others.

St. Patrick's Cathedral, built in 1190, is an imposing edifice. The tower is of solid blue limestone, surmounted by a granite spire. The cathedral is built in the early English or pointed style of architecture. In it are the monuments of many celebrated persons. The other historical church is Christ Church, which is one hundred and fifty years older than the cathedral. In it Richard II. conferred knighthood upon four Irish kings. The impostor Simnell was crowned in it as Edward VI., the crown used for the occasion being one that rested upon the head of the statue of the Virgin, and taken from the Church of St. Mary.

The streets of Dublin are well looked after. The most attractive is called Sackville, one hundred and twenty feet wide; on it are the post-office and Nelson's pillar. On the latter are engraved the names of the prominent victories of the Admiral. The shaft is seventy-two feet high with a capital of seven feet, on the top of which is a colossal statue of Lord Nelson leaning against the capstan of a vessel. The column is hollow, containing a stairway, so that it can be ascended. There are also statues, in other parts of the city, of William III. and the four Georges.

Phœnix Park, situated upon the river, contains nearly two thousand acres, and is seven miles in circumference. All through it are scattered magnificent elms. The Phœnix Pillar is of Portland stone and has on the top a phœnix upon its funeral pyre, with wings outspread.

The Wellington testimonial is a shaft two hundred feet high,—resembling Cleopatra's needle. On it, in bas-relief medallions, are the names of all the victories won by the Duke of Wellington. The grass in the park is so thickly set, that the footprints of the horses cannot be seen. We rode around the city in a jaunting car, which is an ugly, uncomfortable, two-wheeled vehicle, the passengers sitting back to back. The roads, however, are as smooth as a tenpin alley, and not barred by toll-gates.

## By Boat and Rail. 117

We visited the world-renowned Guinness brewery, where they turn out two thousand hogsheads of beer a day, and waste more than the ordinary breweries make. The beer can be seen running over the floor in streams.

The country around Dublin is highly cultivated. We never saw a finer grass-growing country. It grows everywhere, even on the stone fences, which are concealed by it. The cattle stand in it up to their knees, and it is not unusual to cut three crops in a year. The cows are good, round, and plump, and a choice one costs a hundred dollars, which is a peasant's fortune. We have seen some of their hunting horses, which are, as Shakespeare says:

"Long-hoof'd, short-jointed, fetlocks shag and long,
  Broad breast, full eyes, small head, and nostril wide,
  High crest, short ears, straight legs and passing strong,
  Thin mane, thick tail, broad buttocks, tender hide."

## CHAPTER XXIV.

FROM Dublin we went to Cork, which is partially built upon the mainland, and partially on an island at the mouth of the river Lee. As it is the head-quarters of the southern military district of Ireland, there is always a large garrison there, composed of English and Scottish soldiers. Cork is also the seat of the courts for the southern part of the island, and is therefore a place of considerable importance. The harbor is so large that, it is said, the entire British navy could find a safe anchorage. The city is one of the greatest manufacturing places in Ireland, and thousands of vessels from all parts of the world visit it every year. The surrounding country is undulating, and the coast indented with a great number of bays.

Southwest from Cork, thirteen miles, is the town of Kinsale, and four miles from it is the Old Head of Kinsale, a high promontory projecting three miles into the Atlantic Ocean.

On this high and dangerous rock is a lighthouse, which can be seen twenty miles away. This warning light was not on the headland in 1822, when my father was wrecked there on the night of April 22d, on which occasion every cabin passenger on the packet ship *Albion*, bound from New York to Liverpool, was drowned except himself. Securing a single foothold, he clung to a perpendicular rock, which rose two hundred feet above him. Here he remained for several hours, with the spray of the angry waves dashing over him. As soon as it was light the people descended the rocks as far as they could, and dropped him a rope, which he fastened around his body and was drawn to a place of safety. He was taken to the hospitable mansion of Mr. James B. Gibbons, where he lay for several weeks, receiving every attention.

After viewing the scene where this disaster occurred, we returned to Kinsale, and from there we went to the renowned lakes of Killarney. They resemble the Mirror Lakes of the Yosemite Valley, though much larger. A member of Parliament owns the land around these lakes. His park is filled with game, and his stud of horses and pack of hounds are considered the best in Ireland. The hounds in England have a good nose, but those of our country surpass them in tongue and foot.

On the occasion of our visit to the lakes the weather was disagreeable, being very wet and cold, consequently our stay was of short duration. On our trips through Ireland we noticed many trees and flowers similar to those found in the United States. The shamrock, which is similar to clover, grows with vigor. There are fewer birds in Ireland than in America, but they have the skylark, one of the sweetest songsters, which poises in its upward flight and fills the air with melody.

Ireland is a good country for the rich man, but a bad one for the poor man. The Irish people seem to be happy, for they are always in a good humor and full of natural wit, which indicates that they all have some time in life made a pilgrimage to Blarney Castle and kissed the famous stone. They are also ready with their shillalahs, and will crack a crown with the same good humor as they do their jokes.

It is said of the inhabitants of the United Kingdom: "An Englishman is never happy but when he is miserable ; a Scotchman is never at home but when he is abroad ; and an Irishman is never at peace but when he is fighting."

From Killarney we proceeded to Queenstown, and took steamer for our native land.

## CHAPTER XXV.

SHORTLY after the opening of the Union Pacific Railroad an excursion across the continent was given, of which we availed ourselves. We stopped at several points of interest. It is not necessary to describe any of the cities or the country between the Atlantic coast and Omaha, as they were even at that time not considered in the wild and woolly West. At the time of the trip Omaha was a frontier town of about twenty-five hundred inhabitants, whereas now it is a busy city of one hundred and forty thousand, the old frontier town having given way to modern improvements.

Cheyenne, one of the stations on the route, having at that time three or four hundred inhabitants, is now the capital of Wyoming. The journey was through a sparsely settled country to Ogden, where we left the main line and went down to Salt Lake City, the Jerusalem of the Mormons—with a population of fifty thousand. It is situated on the banks of the Jordan River, which connects Lake Utah, a fresh-water lake, with Salt Lake. In this particular there is a resemblance to the Holy Land, with its fresh-water Sea of Galilee and the Dead Sea.

The city is laid out with streets crossing each other at right angles, one hundred and thirty feet in width. The houses are all set back twenty feet from the street, the intervening space being planted with trees and shrubbery. On each side of the streets streams of clear water flow, used to irrigate the lawns and gardens. The great attractions of Salt Lake City are the Mormon Tabernacle, the Temple, the Endowment House, and the Tithing House. The first is an oval structure two hundred and thirty feet long, one hundred and thirty, wide, and seventy, high. This great assembly-room will seat eight or ten thousand persons, and is the largest place of worship in America. On the day of our visit, which was Sunday, the Sacrament was administered. Great baskets of bread, and silver tankards filled with water instead of wine, were placed upon tables, before which stood the bishops, who broke the bread and passed it and the water to the vast multitude.

On our first visit the foundations of the temple, which was in course of construction, were level with the ground, the walls being sixteen feet in thickness. It is not the intention of the Mormons to use this as a place of ordinary Sunday worship, but to use it on special occasions, taking the place of the Endowment House, where all who enter the faith are initiated into the mysteries of Mormonism.

In the tabernacle there is a magnificent organ, which is the largest in America. Mr. Drexel, of Philadelphia, who was one of the party, was permitted to perform upon the instrument. The acoustic properties of the tabernacle are so perfect that the slightest whisper can be heard in any part of the building.

On our second visit to Salt Lake City the temple had been built to the square. This edifice when completed will cost about two million dollars.

The Tithing House is managed by the bishops, who take from every Mormon one tenth of his products, the same amount of his

## By Boat and Rail. 125

yearly profits, and exact one tenth of his time for the benefit of the Church. By this system of tithing they get three-tenths of their followers' subsistence. The co-operative store is the great warehouse of the "Saints," in which are gathered the results of the tithing. On our visits to the city we did not see Brigham Young, as he was out of town, but Bishop Hunter, a native of Chester County, politely showed us around.

In the northern part of the city are the warm springs, which are strongly impregnated with sulphurated hydrogen. The water from these springs is conducted to bathing-houses, which are much frequented.

A curious custom prevalent among the "Latter Day Saints" is the painting upon their signs a solitary eye, and the words "Holiness to the Lord." The men, prior to the passage of the law making polygamy a criminal offence against the United States, seemed to have more wives than horses. Outwardly, the plurality of wives appears to have been abolished; but, it is said, the practice is still secretly observed. They seem to be of the same opinion as the Esquimaux, who say a man who has three wives in this world is sure of heaven.

Great Salt Lake is ten or twelve miles to the northwest of the city. It is seventy miles long and thirty, wide, containing several islands. The water is twenty-two per cent. salt. It is so salty that it contains no animal life; and it is so buoyant that a person can float in it with the greatest ease. Upon assuming an upright posture, he will sink only to his shoulders.

Along the shores are small, irregular forms, about the size of eggs, which are composed almost entirely of pure salt, caused by evaporation. The lake is without an outlet. In addition to the Jordan, the Bear River and several smaller streams flow into it. The water is becoming fresher, and the lake is getting larger.

Returning to Salt Lake City, we proceeded back to Ogden, and resumed our journey to the Pacific, stopping off at Stockton, from which place we went to the Yosemite Valley.

## CHAPTER XXVI.

WE left the train at Stockton, and started in stages for the Great Valley, by way of Copperopolis, a town which during the war was thronged with miners and their wagons, and did a thriving business. Its success was due to a rich find of copper ore, which in those days was very valuable; but when we passed through the town the houses were empty and the streets deserted.

From Copperopolis, we continued our journey through Sonora and Chinese Camp.

As we began to ascend the mountain, three or four of the party walked in advance of the stage. On arriving near the summit, we observed several Indians moving about in the bush. Two of them came out, carrying their rifles. On being asked if they had seen any bear, they answered in pantomime, by holding up the index finger and the two little fingers, conveying the idea of a large bear and two cubs.

The Indians inquired of us: "Much men?" My companion excitedly and quickly answered: "There are ten stage loads right near"; at which the Indians responded with a grunt, and disappeared in the brush. One of the party remarked: "We made a narrow escape. Those 'red devils' were not hunting bear, but *hair*."

We observed large coveys of black-crested partridges, and the McCall partridge; the latter named after General George A. McCall, who discovered this variety. We also saw a number of ground-squirrels, which resembled our gray squirrel.

The night brought us to Garrote, consisting of a wayside tavern and two or three houses. While resting for the night, there was a disturbance between some miners, who had taken possession of the bar-room, in the absence of the landlord. Several shots were exchanged between the quarrelling men, and one or two were wounded. In the morning, when we asked about the unpleasantness, it was treated by the residents as merely a little episode, which had been forgotten by them between the time of its occurrence and sunrise.

After breakfast, we mounted our mustangs,

and started for the Yosemite. A colony of yellow-jackets had built their nest in the trail. A greaser boy, who was acting as guide, rode into the nest and stirred them up. Thereupon, they vigorously attacked the head of the procession, and the horses seemed suddenly to have business in an opposite direction. Amid the plunging of the horses and the screaming of the women, the yellow-jackets kept strictly to work, as they were striking for their homes, and had their *firesides* with them. In the excitement, several of the party who had displayed their unskilful horsemanship, in the morning, by mounting on the off-side, of course were thrown; but, lighting on the largest part of their bodies, only sustained a slight concussion.

The trail is through a forest, crossing many small and rapid streams, and the trees are blazed at intervals, so that in winter when the ground is covered with snow, the trail will not be lost. A ride of a day took us into the valley, but now a stage carries passengers directly there.

Yosemite originally belonged to the national government, but was ceded to the State of

California, on condition that it be kept as a public park. It is located on both sides of the Merced River, and is about ten miles long and from a half to two miles wide, walled in on either side by almost perpendicular rocks of granite. It is one of the wonders of the world. Its principal peaks are El Capitan, the Sentinel Dome, the Cap of Liberty, the Cathedral Rocks, and the Cathedral Spires, all of which are remarkable for their height and grandeur. There are a great number of water-falls and cascades, which, in the spring-time, are greatly enlarged by the melting snow. The most notable are Sentinel Falls, Yosemite Falls, and the Bridal Veil. A miller from the State of Delaware remarked, in a sad tone of voice, yet with a keen business eye: "There is enough waste water-power here to turn all the mills of Delaware and Pennsylvania."

In the valley we met Indians with black-tail deer, which they had shot and were carrying on their backs, having their forelegs tied together and passed across their foreheads. They followed us for the little provision which they gathered from our luncheon. They frequent the valley for the purpose of gathering the acorns, which they bury so as to extract the resin. Afterwards they convert them into a paste, from which they manufacture a kind of bread.

From the valley we went to the Big Tree Grove of Calaveras. These trees are grand and awe-inspiring, and you look upon them with astonishment and wonder as they tower towards the sky. They range from 150 to 275 feet in height, and have a diameter from twenty to thirty feet. One of these giants was overthrown by being bored through with augers. The stump was then levelled off and converted into a dancing floor, measuring thirty-two feet over, and capable of accommodating several sets of dancers. The trunk was made into a bowling-alley.

Another of these trees had fallen through age, and left a depression in the ground as large as a mill-race. A third, which had also fallen, was partially decayed in the heart, and, with some assistance from fire, had been made large enough to permit a horse and rider to enter it for about thirty yards. Two of us performed the feat, and, on reaching the terminus, dismounted from our horse, ascended a flight of steps, and crawled through a knot-hole in the side of the tree.

One of these trees, so the scientists say, is three thousand years old. The bark is from fifteen inches to two feet in thickness. A section was removed some years ago from one of the trees, and taken to Europe, where it was put on exhibition.

Having partially satisfied ourselves with these Californian wonders, we returned to Stockton and proceeded to San Francisco.

## CHAPTER XXVII.

SAN FRANCISCO, the New York of the Pacific coast, is built upon the western shore of the Bay of San Francisco, and is reached from the ocean through the Golden Gate. Its population is about three hundred thousand. It is a business metropolis, with wide streets, broken by a large number of squares and parks. The old buildings of the days of '49 have nearly all disappeared, and in their places, houses, stores, and hotels of grand proportions have been erected. Although it is said to be a godless city, it has nearly a hundred churches, several fine libraries, and scores of public buildings. The hotels are good; the leading ones being the Palace, Occidental, Baldwin, and Lick House. The Palace is the largest, occupying a square, and costing $6,000,000. The Lick House was built by James Lick, who was a cabinet-maker in Hanover, York County, Pennsylvania, and settled in California as early as 1847, where he speculated in land. He was a philanthropist, and gave $4,000,000 to public enterprises in San Francisco, besides giving to the State a school for mechanics and arts, which cost $500,000. He also built the famous Lick Observatory, which contains the largest telescope in the world, costing, with its appointments, $1,000,000. Among the attractions of this great city is the Chinese quarter, where everything tends to make one think of Canton or Pekin. The language, signs, and odors are all foreign to the American eye, ear, and nose.

We visited their theatre, in which a play had been in continuous progress for a week and would take weeks more to finish. Upon leaving the theatre, we went to a Mexican restaurant, where we had a lunch, in genuine Mexican style. As that race is very fond of cayenne, it was a highly seasoned one. The meal consisted of three courses, which may be summed up in the words, hot, hotter, hottest. It is even said that wild animals will not eat a dead Mexican, because his flesh is too hot. Other points of interest are the Cliff House and the Seal Rocks, where a number of seals can be seen sporting in the water and basking on the rocks.

Here we took the steamer for home via Panama. The boat was uncomfortably crowded and the weather exceedingly warm, and as we were not attired for a temperature of eighty or ninety degrees in the shade, we suffered considerably. The deck-hands and stewards were nearly all Japanese, who appeared to make very good sailors. The attention of the latter could not be surpassed.

We stopped at Mazatlan and Acapulco, both Mexican cities. At the former, which we reached at mid-day, the temperature was nearly one hundred degrees, and the people appeared to be all enjoying a *siesta*. We looked in a school-house, where the mistress was asleep in a hammock, and the children had followed suit on their benches. Being desirous of purchasing a hammock we entered a store, the proprietor of which was asleep, who, on being awakened, seemed annoyed that we should make a call at such an unseasonable hour. He acted as if he would much rather sleep than sell.

There are no wharves here, and everything is taken to and from the vessels on lighters. A number of cattle was swum from the shore to our steamer, and hoisted on board by fastening a rope around their horns.

Acapulco is the most important port of Mexico on the Pacific, and has the best harbor. From this place large quantities of hides, silver, indigo, and cochineal are shipped. The people are also largely engaged in pearl fishing. After a stop of a few hours we steamed away for Panama.

This city, consisting of about twenty-five thousand inhabitants, is situated on the Bay of Panama, and is the Pacific terminus of the Panama Railroad. It is the capital of the state of Panama, which is one of the most important commonwealths of the United States of Colombia. It is one of the oldest cities in South America, dating back as early as 1500. In its early days it suffered considerably from the ravages of the buccaneers, notably, from the raids made by the famous pirate Morgan, who sacked and burned it. Some old rusty cannon can still be seen lying upon a promontory close to the city. In addition to depredations at the hands of freebooters, it has been burned several times by accidental fires.

At Panama we took the cars for Aspinwall. This railroad was built in 1855, and every cross-tie cost the lives of three men, so unhealthy was the region through which it was constructed. Men of several nationalities were employed on the work, such as Irishmen, Germans, native Indians, Mexicans, and Chinamen, none of whom were able to cope with the climate. Finally the negro was employed with success. The road is forty-six miles long and very crooked, passing through chaparral and tangled forest. The highest point is 250 feet above the sea-level. It cost twenty-five dollars to ride these forty-six miles. Emigrants are prohibited from walking on the road, and it is almost an impossibility to cross the isthmus, through such a tangle, independent of the dangers from wild animals, snakes, and malaria. The cars have blinds instead of glass, and the seats are cane. The stations are erected upon stilts of iron, to protect them from the ravages of the insects, which attack all wood that has been cut. For the same reason, the telegraph poles and cross-ties are made of iron or stone.

Aspinwall, the northern terminus of the railroad, is situated on Manzanilla Island, which has been ceded to the railroad company forever by the United States of Colombia. This city was named after Mr. W. H.

Aspinwall of New York City, who was the projector of the railroad and its first president.

A party of Mexicans bound for New York boarded the steamer at Mazatlan. They had neglected to doff their light summer clothing at Aspinwall, and when we arrived north of Cuba, the air becoming quite cool, the poor fellows huddled close to the steam pipes to keep warm. They could not get at their trunks, and if they had, it was not likely that they had anything more seasonable. When we reached New York it was snowing, and they presented a deplorable appearance, resembling butterflies which had emerged from their cocoons out of season. They went fluttering and shivering to their hacks to be taken to their destination.

## CHAPTER XXVIII.

ON a second trip to the Pacific coast our first stop of any importance was Denver. This city, situated at the foot of the Rocky Mountains, has a population of about one hundred thousand. It is comparatively a new city, and the people are making mud and business fly.

At the time we crossed Kansas it was resplendent with verdure; yet a few years before the grasshoppers had been so numerous and so hungry that they ate everything that was lying around loose. So destructive were they that a farm could have been purchased for a sack of flour and a mule.

From Denver we turned southward, made a brief visit to Colorado Springs, and then proceeded to Manitou, at the base of Pike's Peak. The foot-hills of this peak are higher than Mt. Washington. We rode on horseback high enough to satisfy our curiosity. Now there is a railroad to the summit. We also saw the remarkable "Garden of the Gods," with its riven and distorted rocks. Leaving Manitou, we proceeded over the Denver and Rio Grande Railroad to Pueblo, and thence to Santa Fé by way of Veta Pass. On this road there is a curve called the "Mule Shoe," to construct which the engineers were obliged to build four miles of road to gain an advance of half a mile. Sometimes the engine was going in a directly opposite direction to the rear car of the train it was pulling. At Conejos, before going to Santa Fé, we made a run to Silverton, a town among the clouds and snow, where they have honeycombed the mountains in their search after the bright metal. From what we observed generally we concluded that more money could be made on top of the ground than underneath. At Continental Divide we saw vast herds of cattle and sheep. A gentleman who owned thirty thousand head told us that he had sold ten thousand for forty dollars per head, weighing from eight hundred to nine hundred pounds on the hoof. If the winter is not too hard and no blizzards are encountered they will thrive quite well under the lee of the mountains, and when the spring comes they grow with the grass.

The cattle ranch is the money-making business of the West, as it costs nothing for pasture, and cow-boys can be hired at thirty-five dollars per month and found. In Colorado there is very little rainfall as compared with other localities.

From Silverton we retraced our steps to Conejos, and from there went to Santa Fé. It is one of the oldest towns in the United States, and has a population of ten or fifteen thousand, consisting of all nationalities. The streets are narrow, resembling in that respect the old Spanish cities. The houses are built with adobe; water is scarce, but the air is pure.

Santa Fé, before the railroads were built across the continent, was a very important trading post. The city is not an attractive one, except for its age, and the inhabitants are only remarkable for murdering time. In this city is the oldest church in America, San Miguel, built in 1580. The old palace of the Spanish governors dates back to 1650, and is now occupied by the Historical Society of New Mexico.

From Santa Fé we crossed the territory from north to south. The railroad is constructed in the Rio Grande valley, in which there is some excellent land. The Pueblo Indians cultivate the ground in a primitive way, with a wooden plough and a winding ditch. They are industrious, and, like their burros, make haste slowly. We stopped at Albuquerque, which is a bustling city, some of the inhabitants of which have become rich by shaking and sifting the mountains for treasures. From this point we went to El Paso, where we took the Southern Pacific Railroad for Los Angeles.

There is some fertile country on the route, and some extremely barren. We saw the gold shining in its virgin state; passed through mining towns, which hung on the mountain like bird-cages on a wall, and through cañons which were beyond description of pen or brush. On the Southern Pacific there were a great many towns, like horses, only seven years old, which neither increased in size nor age. At Lotter Gorge a bear was climbing the mountain, while a pair of eagles were making graceful curves between the sun and the snow-capped peaks. There was very little game, as railroads and game are incompatible. A few buck rabbits, prairie dogs, and an occasional antelope showed their heels to the rattling train.

At the stations between El Paso and Tucson, we were welcomed by Apache Indians, who were following the "white man's road," not for our scalps but for our quarters; they were clothed in little but their complexion. They raced their broncos, threw their lassos, danced their war dance, shot their arrows, and scooped in the "filthy lucre" from the innocent "tenderfoot." This tribe is the great unwashed, and is an animated ranche for vermin and filth.

At one of the stations we encountered the "King of the Cow-boys," as they called him. He was dressed in a buckskin hunting-shirt and slashed trousers, with a broad-brimmed hat and rattling spurs. He fairly glittered with knives and pistols, and appeared to be fretting for a fight. We were told not to irritate him, as he had, the day before, slaughtered two innocent men. The ladies looked upon him with amazement and wonder, while the men, with eyes turned one way and toes another, were anxious to leave his company, as he nervously dropped his hand on the silver-mounted butt of a loaded pistol. The exceeding politeness of the men was most absurd, and, on his retirement, they wiped the perspiration from their manly brows. Before we reached the next stopping-place, in walked the dreaded "King of the Cow-boys," but this time he was dressed in his proper uniform, which was that of a baggage-master. The passengers laughed at the deception which had been practised upon them, and paid well for the joke; for his real occupation was not that of smashing heads, but trunks.

From Tucson to Yuma the country was barren, covered with sand, cacti of immense size, and sage bush; as there is scarcely any rainfall in this section of the country, it is exceedingly dry, and the land is killed with thirst; the only indication of moisture we observed in crossing this desert was an individual with a corkscrew. Yuma is the hottest place in the United States. The sun, instead of being millions of miles away, seemed to be almost within reach, and the inhabitants appeared to be mostly in "the melting mood."

After crossing the Colorado River the country was a desert until we reached the

Cajon Pass, whence the route to Los Angeles was through a beautiful and fertile district, here and there, covered with palm, lemon, almond, olive, and pepper trees. We finally reached Los Angeles, which is the handsomest city of Southern California, and is in the great vine-growing district.

## CHAPTER XXIX.

LOS ANGELES, a city of about fifty thousand inhabitants, is situated in a valley and on a river of the same name. It is in the centre of the great fruit belt, and has been well named, surrounded as it is by rich pastures, extensive fruit orchards, and ever-blooming flower gardens. The orange-trees were full to excess, the air was laden with perfume of fruit and flower, and the heavy-headed and bending grain promised an abundant harvest. Added to this is a most genial climate, which makes it a place you regret to leave. There are nearly twenty miles of macadamized streets on which there are cable and electric street-cars.

Nine miles distant is Pasadena, a city famous for its attractive villas. We visited the ranch of Mr. Rose, where we saw cows worth their weight in silver, and horses valued at thirty thousand dollars. Returning to Los Angeles, we went to Santa Monica, a seaside resort of

Los Angeles about twenty miles distant. Like Long Branch, the shore is abrupt and fast land to the flood, the vegetation growing luxuriantly to the very ocean. Here we caught plenty of fish, some of which were viviparous. Returning to the "City of Angels" we resumed our journey northward, passing through the western edge of the Mojave Desert, and through the celebrated Tehachapi Pass. This road is the most serpentine that has ever been constructed, and on one of the curves the road actually crosses itself, one road-bed being eighty feet above the other, which is spanned by a bridge. It takes a day and a night to go from Los Angeles to San Francisco.

From San Francisco we journeyed to Monterey, the great seaside resort of the San Franciscans. The Hotel del Monte is the property of the railroad company, and has seven thousand acres attached. The company has spared neither pains nor money upon the property, and, with the assistance of nature, has made it very attractive and comfortable. The grounds are artistically laid out, with lakes, fountains, groves, and well macadamized roads. Hundreds of Chinamen are engaged constantly in keeping the grounds in perfect condition. It is said that a million dollars has been expended upon this hotel property.

Quitting Monterey we returned to San Francisco through the Santa Clara valley, which is a very highly cultivated country, rich in cereals and fruits. Magnificent houses abound, with every indication of wealth; for the valley is the home of the "bonanza kings."

Immense crops are raised in California, some ranches turning out a hundred thousand dollars' worth of grain annually. Sixty bushels of wheat to the acre is not an uncommon yield, and at times the wheat crop has reached forty millions of bushels. Large quantities of barley are cut green and fed to the stock instead of hay. Alfalfa, a kind of clover, which was introduced from Chili, is a very important crop. It grows luxuriantly, and is cut four or five times a year, aggregating from eight to ten tons per acre. Corn is rarely planted. The temperature varies but slightly throughout the year, and averages about seventy-five degrees. Some of the ranchmen plough, harrow, and sow their grain at the same time, driving ten horses to the harrow. We saw eight reaping-machines in a field of barley. Fruit grows abundantly, grapes being one of the staple crops. The vines are cut off a few feet from the ground and support themselves, some of the vines being half a foot in diameter; cherries, strawberries, and apricots are unusually large and perfect in form, but somewhat insipid.

Food is cheap and good. Fish and oysters are plenty. Shad has been introduced from the Atlantic coast. The butter was excellent, reminding us of the rich pasture of Chester County. Stock here is choice, but high in price. A good horse, as elsewhere, brings his full value, nevertheless one can buy a bucking bronco for a few dollars, which will give you more business and exercise than any investment that is quoted on the market.

While in San Francisco we rode behind the celebrated horse "John Stewart," that has made his twenty miles an hour, and was considered the best roadster in America. He was then owned by the late Dr. Brunner, who was formerly a resident of Chester County. We returned home by way of Salt Lake City, of which mention has been made in a preceding chapter.

## CHAPTER XXX.

PRINCE EDWARD ISLAND lies in the Gulf of St. Lawrence, north of Nova Scotia. The sea route from Boston to this island gives the visitor the opportunity of stopping at Halifax, the capital of the province of Nova Scotia, the harbor of which is extensive, and one of the most commodious in the world.

The route to Prince Edward Island is through the Gut of Canso, which separates Nova Scotia from Cape Breton Island. The current of the Gut of Canso is exceedingly rapid, and its passage is attended with some danger at certain seasons of the year.

Prince Edward Island is about one hundred and thirty miles long, and from four to thirty-five, wide. Its chief city, Charlottestown, where we landed, has a population of about ten thousand. While in Charlottestown a show made a street parade, which was rather an uncommon occurrence in that town. As the procession was passing a bank, all hands left their figures and money to witness it. At the same time a man asked the president of the bank if he could throw into the cellar a load of coal that was lying on the pavement. The request was granted. When the clerks balanced the accounts in the evening they were fifteen thousand dollars short. The innocent looking coal-heaver had gone through the bank, and the officials had "seen the elephant."

The island is well watered by a number of streams, in which there is good trout fishing. Francis Jacobs, one of our party, a skilful angler, who can cast a fly so as to drop in the desired spot, "as light as falls the flaky snow," soon filled his creel with the "speckled beauties." The land is fertile, and the principal crops are potatoes, oats, wheat, and barley. The people have large herds of cattle, sheep, and pigs, but those of the coast line are chiefly engaged in fishing, catching large quantities of cod, mackerel, and alewives.

While there we went mackerel fishing. The bait, consisting of ground fish, is continually thrown out of the boat, until a school of mackerel strikes the floating bait and follows it up to its source. Then, throwing out your baited hooks, you can make a good catch.

On our return a fog suddenly dropped on the bay, so thick that we lost both our bearings and our tempers. As we had only an "ash breeze," it was near morning before we heard the sound of the bugle, played by our friend, who had become anxious for our safety. This told us the direction of home.

Prince Edward is a very healthy place, and, though the summers are short, the winters are not excessively severe. The island was once heavily timbered, but lumbering and fires have made great gaps in the primeval forests. Living is cheap. A native told us that he kept his family comfortably on a pension of two hundred dollars, which he received from the English government.

Leaving Prince Edward Island, we crossed Northumberland Strait to Shediac, in New Brunswick, and proceeded to St. John by rail. This city is located at the mouth of the St. John River which empties into the Bay of Fundy. This bay is remarkable for its exceeding high tides, which, at its upper end, rise to the height of seventy feet, and rush in with such rapidity

## By Boat and Rail. 153

that animals are frequently overtaken and drowned.

Returning to the States, we proceeded to the White Mountains, where we ascended Mt. Washington, which is six thousand two hundred feet high. The grandeur of the scenery surrounding this group has given this portion of New Hampshire the title of the "American Switzerland." There is a railroad to the summit of Mt. Washington. The cars are furnished with cog-wheels, and there is a middle rail with teeth, into which the cogs work on the same principle as any geared machinery. There is also an arrangement attached, which will not let the train run backward, so the danger of any break of the locomotive renders the ascent very safe. When the bill was before the New Hampshire legislature to construct this road, a member who was opposed to it remarked that it would be as practicable to build a railroad to the moon.

The Summit House and United States Signal Service Office are fastened down to the mountain by chain cables, so that storms cannot blow them away. It is rare that a view of any duration can be had from the summit, on account of the almost continual mist; occasionally, however, a glimpse for a few minutes of the other mountains and the valleys can be obtained through a rift in the fog and clouds. The descent of the mountain is exciting and enjoyable, but it is not so thrilling as the ascent and descent of some of the peaks in the Rocky Mountains.

# CHAPTER XXXI.

QUEBEC, the only walled city in North America, might be very properly called a French city with English masters. It was settled by the French in 1534, but in 1759 was conquered by England. Its French population has adhered with tenacity to the tongue of its mother country, and has not wandered from the faith of the Roman Catholic Church. A few miles from the city we met people who could only speak the French language. We were told that there was only one negro in Quebec, and he had concluded to leave before the winter set in, as it took all he made to keep him warm.

The city is divided into two parts, called the upper and the lower towns. The former, on a high promontory called Cape Diamond, is surrounded by a wall. At the extremity of Cape Diamond is the citadel, which is the strongest fortress in America, from which fact the city is frequently called the "Gibraltar of

America." Back from the town are the Plains of Abraham, where General Wolfe won his victory over the French under Montcalm, and lost his life. During the American Revolution the Colonial army, led by Montgomery, made an attempt to capture the city from the English. The American General had about one thousand New York soldiers, and before making the assault he addressed them as follows: "Men of New York, you will not fear to follow where your General leads." At the first volley from the enemy's musketry Montgomery fell, mortally wounded.

The lower town is at the base of Cape Diamond, the rocks having been cut away to make room for the houses. This is the commercial portion of Quebec, while the upper town is principally devoted to residences and public edifices. In the vicinity of the lower town, along the river banks, are large ship-building establishments and commodious floating docks. The principal business is the timber trade, and immense rafts are floated down the Ottawa and other rivers from the great interior forests. Millions of feet of lumber are sent annually out of the St. Lawrence River from

Quebec. The Falls of Montmorency, a short distance away, are two hundred and fifty feet high—much superior to and grander than those of Minnehaha (Laughing Water) near Minneapolis, which are but forty feet high and only made celebrated by the *Song of Hiawatha*, From Quebec we went to Montreal, and then to the Thousand Islands, which are interesting. They are the largest collection of islands in the world. The passage through the rapids, —the "Long Sault," the "Cedars," and the "Lachine"—is most thrilling. The steamer rushes through them under the guidance of a skilful Caughnawaga Indian.

Returning to Montreal, we took the Canadian Pacific Railroad for Victoria. This is the most northern railroad route across the American continent, and one of the five great iron belts which connect the Atlantic with the Pacific. It was constructed with English capital, and completed in 1887. It is a single track the entire distance of thirty-two hundred miles, but differs from the English roads in having the United States system of cars and locomotives, the latter having covered cabs for the engineers, which the English locomotives do not have. The trip is made in about seven days. The road was an inexpensive one until they struck the Rocky Mountains. In some localities it is perfectly straight for the distance of forty miles, not even having a bridge or an embankment. The country along the road is composed of forest, prairie, and mountain. For the first thousand miles it is a wilderness in every sense of the word, but not a howling one, as we neither saw nor heard an animal or bird. It was as silent as the sky above. The endless stretch of pines was stunted and worthless. The soil appeared to be thin. The next thousand miles were composed almost entirely of prairie, which was rolling and fertile, and on which good crops of wheat, oats, and barley were raised. It is too cold in this latitude for corn-growing. For miles and miles we rode along without seeing a habitation, and the eye grew weary looking at the long undulating plains, which seemed to reach to the bending clouds. A few wild flowers—the rose, the red lobelia, and the trembling bluebells—relieved the monotony. Along this part of the route we saw a few animals, such as the gray wolf, the badger, and the coyote, which would

## By Boat and Rail. 159

leisurely trot off as the train approached, until they were lost beyond "the divide." The little prairie-dogs would appear and disappear in their burrows with wonderful activity. Wild ducks were floating on the ponds among the water-lilies with their broods, and occasionally a bunch of antelope might be seen stretching their graceful forms in wonder at the swiftly passing train. The buffaloes, which so recently blackened these prairies and rolled in the rich pasture, have all been destroyed, and the only signs they have left are their interlaced trails, while their bones whiten the green and solitary surface. The Indians still remain, and their wigwams are pitched about the stations. They are dignified and stand like statues, wrapped in red blankets, and, with stolid countenance, seem to read their downfall in the progress of civilization.

When we reached the Rocky Mountains the road twisted and turned like a snake. It climbs high mountains and almost perpendicular cliffs, winds through cañons, descends into deep gorges, burrows into long tunnels, and crosses swift rivers—truly a grand piece of engineering. On this trip, which was in the summer, the snow was melting on the peaks, and came tumbling down in white streams as if from the clouds. The rivers had become so swollen, and some of the bridges had been so seriously damaged, that on one occasion we were obliged to leave the cars, walk over a bridge, and take another train. It was not an agreeable or easy task to accomplish, with a roaring river beneath and a bridge swinging from the force of the water. We were well satisfied when we stepped from the last tie upon *terra firma*.

The road crosses the heads of the Columbia, Frazer, Thompson, and Kicking Horse rivers. The Frazer River was fifty feet higher than usual, and gurgled between narrow, perpendicular rocks three hundred feet below the track. It rushed along with such terrific force that it appeared to be running on its edge.

The one disagreeable and annoying feature of the trip was the mosquitoes, which were so numerous and so intent on their business that they came early and stayed late; the natives say that they come and depart on snow-shoes.

After a continuous ride of seven days we reached Victoria, the capital of British Columbia, on Vancouver Island. The city has a population of about fifteen thousand inhabitants, of which four thousand are the almond-eyed Chinese and one thousand, Indians, the balance being a mixture of different nationalities. The streets of the city are wide and well paved, and the dwellings are set back from the street, with yards in front, in which flowers bloom nearly all the year.

The island of Vancouver is two hundred miles long, and varies from thirty to fifty, in width. The greater part of the island is mountainous, with peaks from eight to nine thousand feet in height. Mount Arrowsmith is the highest, being an almost perpendicular mass of rock rising from the shore, which might be compared to Mount Washington, though it has not risen to the dignity of a signal-service station, nor is it reached by a railroad. The island is densely wooded, containing much valuable timber, such as the white fir, the Douglas pine, and the cedar, some of which grow to the height of three hundred feet. The last two are largely used in ship and canoe building. Coal has also been found on the island in large quantities.

The climate is cold and the summer is short,

but very hot. There is an abundance of wild fowl and wild animals, such as the bear, wolf, puma, and deer. The island is a great fishing depot, salmon, cod, herring, and halibut being abundant, and forming one of the chief features of business and traffic.

Vancouver's Island was discovered in 1762 by Captain Vancouver, of the British Navy. The city of Victoria was founded in 1857, at which time the great rush was made to the British Columbia gold-fields. It is now a province of the Dominion of Canada, and a representative of the colonial government resides at Victoria. At the time of our arrival the people were celebrating the fiftieth anniversary of Queen Victoria's reign. It was done with sham battles, boat-racing, fire-works, and other amusements. We came over from the mainland in a boat loaded with soldiers, and if they attacked the enemy with half the zeal that they did the victuals, they would soon annihilate them. We had to wait for the fourth table before getting what little was left.

## CHAPTER XXXII.

THE trip from Victoria to Sitka, Alaska, is made entirely by water, surpassing in grandeur and scenic beauty anything that one can imagine or describe. The route was what is termed the inside passage—that is, between the mainland and the numerous islands between it and the ocean. We steamed up a narrow channel along Vancouver Island a distance of two hundred miles, with towering mountains on either side, covered with cedar, hemlock, and spruce, which shut out the swell and storm of the Pacific and rendered the water as smooth as that of a lake. The channel is in a labyrinth of islands with quiet bays into which empty numerous streams. From the northern extremity of Vancouver to Queen Charlotte Island there is a stretch of a hundred miles entirely open to the sea. We then entered Fitzhugh Sound, shut in by the mainland on the east and by the islands on the west, above which Mount Buxton rises like a needle, thirty-four hundred feet high. In some places the way was so narrow that one could almost bathe one's hand in the foaming cascades and reach the ferns upon the banks. The water was so clear that the trees, rocks, and sky were reflected upon the surface like a painting. We saw but little life in this "thrilling region of thick-ribbed ice." Now and then an Indian canoe would glide by and disappear with its occupant behind an island, or an eagle sail screaming among the cliffs and crags. An occasional whale spouted in the distance, and some seal played among the floating ice. Grenville Channel, which connects Wright's Sound with Chatham Sound, is perfectly straight for fifty miles, and lies between Pitt Island and the mainland. After entering Chatham Sound we obtained another view of the ocean. Up to this point we had been entirely in English waters, but after crossing latitude 54° and 40', which is just north of Dundas Island and south of Prince of Wales Island, we entered upon the waters of the United States and within the jurisdiction of the Territory of Alaska. We then passed into Clarence Strait, filled with small islands. This strait is a hun-

## By Boat and Rail. 165

dred miles long and nowhere over four, wide. At the upper end of this passage is Fort Wrangell, which was our first stop, nearly seven hundred miles from Victoria. Fort Wrangell is an old Russian trading-post, and here we had the opportunity of seeing the famous totem poles of the Indians. Some of these poles are sixty feet high, curiously carved, and frequently ornamented with a figure on top, wearing a singular-shaped hat. Some of the faces, which are carved on the posts, are most hideous; but whether the poles are intended for luck or worship, no one seems to know. From Fort Wrangell we proceeded northward, passing through Souchoi Channel, and thence into Prince Frederick Sound. Into this sound flows an immense glacier, which has been named Patterson glacier. We next entered the Straits of Stephens, and then through Gastineaux Channel to Juneau. This town, two hundred miles north of Fort Wrangell, is the principal mining centre of Alaska, having one of its ten post-offices. Opposite the town is Douglas Island, on which is one of the largest gold mines in America, having two hundred and forty stamps; the output, it is said, being over $150,000 per month. The gold ore in this mine, the Treadwell, is valued at five times the sum that the United States paid Russia for the Territory.

From Juneau our steamer proceeded up Lynn Canal, a bay of about sixty miles, to Chilkaht Inlet, and stopped at the town of Haines, about a hundred miles above Juneau. It was the most northern point we visited, being in latitude 59°, and nearly a thousand miles from Victoria. The thermometer stood at 45°. The nights in the summer are short, and it is easy to read a newspaper on the deck of the steamer at eleven o'clock. There is a school for the Indian children here under the care of a lady. The Indians resemble the Japanese, and there is no doubt but that they are descended from the Antipodes. As there is a chain of islands between Japan and Alaska, it would have required but little nautical skill for the Japanese to sail from island to island, until they reached the coast of Alaska.

Lynn Canal and Chilkaht Inlet are bounded on either side by high mountains, and from every ravine there flows a glacier of greater or less magnitude. The largest are Eagle and

Davidson. Returning down the canal to Icy Strait, we turned westward and passed through Glacier Bay, into which flows the great Muir glacier. The continual falling of the large icebergs into the water caused the ship to rock like a cradle, and the unceasing cracking and tumbling of the masses of ice reminded one of the roar of battle. The Muir glacier is entirely different from what one would imagine, being really more like a frozen river, blocked and forced upon either side by high mountains, with a front upon the sea of one mile, and from two to three hundred feet high. It is being gradually pushed down its channel, and immense pieces are continually breaking off and falling into the bay. As it recedes into the country it grows wider and thicker, being fed by nearly thirty smaller glacier streams. Its entire length is unknown, though it has been explored for seventy miles inland ; still beyond is seen the same ridge of ice, with towering pinnacles, fantastic in form and dazzling in the sun. We made soundings of one hundred fathoms and found no bottom.

We took on board a supply of ice from this great American ice-house, though there is still enough left to cool all the water and blood of the nation. We have seen glaciers in Switzerland, but they were merely icicles in comparison with this one.

Steaming out of Glacier Bay, we returned through Icy Strait along the coast of Chicagoff Island to Peril Strait, thence down Pogibshi Channel to Sitka, the capital of Alaska. It has a population of about two thousand, of whom more than half are Indians. A gunboat and a force of soldiers are stationed there. There is a Greek church, a relic of the former owners of the country, and a Presbyterian mission with three hundred Indian children. The Episcopalians, the Catholics, and other denominations have planted mission stations, not only at Sitka, but at other points in the Alaskan Territory. The Indian children do very well if kept from the woods, but if they get a sniff of nature they are off, and, like escaped birds, soon become wild. Nostalgia is a disease to which the Indians are subject. They live in shanties, and, if the space is large enough, several families occupy the same room. The fireplace is in the middle of the hut, and answers a twofold purpose—to smoke their fish and warm their bodies. There is a hole in the roof for the exit of the smoke, but most of it lingers with the occupants. The green pelts, the grease, the fish, and a good deal of Indian form a mixture of nauseating smells, which compels you to make a sudden exit and to take the air *straight*.

The squaw here appears to be the "boss." She carries the money, the club, and the tongue, and paddles the canoe, while the "noble red man" wastes his strength in steering. She also saws the wood, while her lazy mate smokes his pipe in peace. When she is dressed in full array, she may be a thing of joy but not of beauty. She has rings in her nose and ears, a tube runs through her lip, her teeth and face are black, she is wrapped in a blanket covered with shirt buttons, and a dirty papoose is slung on her back, yet she walks as if proud of her property and stock.

The natives make their canoes by burning and digging out the inside of the yellow cedar, and are models of symmetry, lightness, and strength. Some of these boats will carry sixty persons and ride the roughest sea. The natives fish more than they hunt, using a hook of their own make, which is a curiosity and a puzzle, with which they catch fish in great abundance. The natives still flatten some of their children's heads by placing them between boards, and build huts over their bodies when they die.

There are large quantities of fish in the Alaskan waters, the principal varieties being rock-cod, flounder, tomcod, white fish, and many species that have only scientific, native, or Russian names. Alaska is not wanting in birds, as many of those found in more southern latitudes are here. Among the most prominent birds that may be mentioned are ptarmigans, magpies, eider ducks, swans, humming-birds, albatrosses, petrels, grebes, ducks, geese, auks, pigeons, wrens, warblers, martins, and ravens. Among the water animals are seals, walruses, and otters; on the land there are bears, deer, elk, moose, caribou, porcupines, wolves, and silver foxes; the pelts of the last mentioned are worth from sixty to seventy-five dollars each. There are also immense forests, which furnish excellent timber. For agricultural purposes the country is too much humped, and there is little in farming because a pumpkin would have to be tied to keep it from rolling

# By Boat and Rail. 171

down hill, and a fire to be built to keep it warm. They have ten months of winter and two of frost. When you talk of winter lingering in the lap of spring, it would have no show in this country, for spring has no lap to spare.

Alaska is one sixth the size of the United States, and was purchased in 1868 from Russia for $7,500,000. From Attu, the most western of the Aleutian chain of islands, to the eastern boundary of the Territory, its extent is equal to the distance from Washington, D. C. to San Francisco. And from north to south, the distance is about the same as from Maine to Florida. Alaska has the highest mountain on the North American continent, Mt. St. Elias, 19,500 feet. It also has one of the longest rivers in the world, the Yukon, which is over three thousand miles long and navigable for two thousand miles. While here, the salmon, which are anadromous, had commenced to run, and the fishermen were expecting a good catch. At the time of the negotiations for the purchase of Alaska, it was said by the late W. H. Seward, Secretary of State, that it was impossible for a ship to land on account of the salmon. They are still so abundant in the spawning season that in the mountain streams they can be thrown out with a pitchfork.

The Indian has an infatuation for killing every kind of animal that he sees, from a squirrel to a bear. He kills in and out of season.

From Sitka, we returned by the inside passage, landing again at Fort Wrangell. It was on the "glorious Fourth," and the day was properly celebrated with sports and speeches. The most interesting of the sports was boat-racing by the Indians. Each canoe contained from fifteen to twenty aboriginals, who propelled their craft with paddles instead of oars. It was astonishing with what rapidity they could drive a canoe through the water. Sometimes it seemed as if they fairly lifted it from the surface. The victorious crew were received by their squaws with rapture. Our party supplied the orators of the day, who astonished the natives more by their gesticulations than by their eloquence, judging from the remark of one of them, who evidently did not understand a word that was uttered. The orator was at the height of his peroration; he had his eyes fixed upon the ceiling, and was vociferating, as if the audience were on top of the roof, while he slashed the air with his arms, stamped the floor, and with burning eloquence made the American Eagle *sore*. It was too much for Mr. Indian, who touched me with his pipe stem, and whispered, "White man much mad, big squaw."

From Victoria we went to Port Townsend, and took steamer for San Francisco. The voyage was not an agreeable one, as the boat was overcrowded, and its freight was largely made up of pelts which were not as sweet as "Cytherea's breath." Three passengers were compelled to occupy a room which was scarcely large enough for one. The sea was rough and choppy, and most of the passengers were sick, The stranger, who assisted my companion and myself in occupying our state-room, appeared to be laboring under the impression that he had eaten something which had disagreed with his stomach, as most of his time was devoted to trying to correct that idea. But it was not surprising, as many of the passengers belonged to the great plains and saw but little water, and it was said to be impossible to get some of them on a boat without first putting their heads in a sack.

## CHAPTER XXXIII.

AFTER a brief stay in the metropolis of the Pacific coast, we took the Mount Shasta Railroad for Portland, twenty-five miles of which were not completed. That distance therefore had to be traversed in stage-coaches, of which there were five with six horses to each. The dust, heat, and rough road made it a journey long to be remembered. We have had some experience with bucking horses, but on this occasion it was a bucking stage. It was impossible to appreciate the scenery, as the eye could not be kept long enough on an object to tell a rock from a cow. A loving couple, who were gotten up in the *dernier mode*, resplendent with shining silk hat, and bonnet, adorned with flowers and birds, occasioned our sympathy; for the lurching and pitching of the stage soon reduced the beauty and symmetry of their head-gear to the things that were. When we got to the railroad, the journey became more pleasant and the scenery grand and beautiful.

The broad and rich Sacramento Valley gleamed with waving grain, and the golden harvest was thick upon level and slope, as far as the eye could reach; while Mount Shasta, 14,500 feet high, with its head in the clouds, and a white mantle upon its shoulders, appeared grand in the distance.

Portland, on the Willamette River, fifteen miles from its juncture with the Columbia River, at the head of ship-navigation, is the largest city in the State, having a population of seventy thousand, is a thorough business place, and one of the wealthiest towns in the Union. One hundred persons worth a million dollars each, reside there. Portland does a tremendous shipping trade through the Columbia River, shipping annually millions of bushels of wheat and thousands of barrels of flour to China and along the American coast. The canning of salmon and the fur trade are carried on to a great extent.

At Portland we took the Northern Pacific Railroad, which runs close to the Columbia River for about two hundred miles through a very fertile section of country, to Walla Walla. Thence we proceeded to Spokane, the most phenomenal city of the Northwest, both in its rapid growth and from a business point of view. A few miles after crossing into Idaho we reached Pend d'Oreille Lake, but the mosquitoes had possession of the ranch, and as we did not wish to occupy their valuable time, we left on the next train for the National Park. The road followed the Clarke's Fork of the Columbia River, through a rough and wild country into the State of Montana. At Livingstone, we left the Northern Pacific Railroad and took the branch to Cinnabar, at the entrance of the National Park, where this road terminates. For a week we viewed this magnificent park. It is sixty-five miles long, fifty-five wide, and contains 3,312 square miles. The entire park is composed of serrated mountains, beautiful valleys, sombre forests, meadows bright with streams and flowers, foaming cascades, awful cañons, placid lakes, and nearly four thousand geysers and hot springs. The wonderful geysers make the earth tremble by their rumbling, and, at intervals, throw into the air columns of boiling water to the height of three hundred feet. The most prominent geysers are the " Excelsior," " Monarch," " Old Faithful,"

"The Minute-Men," and the "Growler." The steam from the " Excelsior," which is the largest geyser in the world, ascends a thousand feet. The hot springs, of which a thousand can be found in the space of a mile square, vary in temperature from 152° to 182°. The mud-pools present every variety of shade and color and are constantly bubbling and seething. Aside from the geysers, the most curious objects are the " Paint Pots," of fantastic designs and colors. The air in the Geyser Basin is thick with steam and sulphurous gases.

In places where the heat is quite perceptible, the ground shakes beneath your feet and seems as if it might, at any moment, burst its thin crust and open the hollow earth. The cañon of the Yellowstone, with its falls of over three hundred feet, its dashing river, its yellow walls towering to the clouds, its crags and rocks shivered by the elements, is one of the most wonderful freaks of nature, and you are awe-stricken by its sublimity and grandeur.

There is plenty of game in the park, but shooting is not allowed. In consequence of this protection, deer stood in the roadways looking at us without fear, and grouse were as tame as chickens. Elk and buffalo were occasionally seen. Once we saw a bear come very near the kitchen of the hotel, and the cook told us that this particular fellow had become quite familiar, for he danced around and wanted the best that was in the shop. Fishing is permitted and some fine catches are made. There are places where trout can be caught and cooked without moving one's position or taking the fish from the hook. They are taken from the sparkling stream and then swung over into a boiling spring. The government is having good roads constructed through the park, and has admirable accommodations for its guests.

Returning, we continued our trip on the Northern Pacific through Montana, North Dakota, and Minnesota to Duluth. These States are being rapidly populated; yet there are millions of acres in which a furrow has never been turned, only waiting for the "seed-time and harvest." At Duluth, "the City of an Unsalted Sea," we embarked for Buffalo via the Great Lakes. The voyage through the lakes was the most delightful water trip we experienced. The Strait of St.

Mary, which connects Lake Superior with Lake Huron, is sixty-three miles long and filled with rapids. The most prominent of these is the Sault Sainte Marie, having a descent of twenty-two feet to the mile. A ship canal has been built around the "Sault," which is the largest of any of its kind, being one third of a mile long, all of solid masonry, twenty-five feet high, and ten feet thick at the base. The gates of the locks are forty feet wide, and the canal is one hundred feet wide, with a depth of twelve feet. Steamers do not go through the "Sault," but Indians run their canoes through it, the passage being attended with much excitement. After passing the straits, the voyage is continued through Lakes Huron and St. Clair into Lake Erie, to Buffalo and Niagara Falls.

## CHAPTER XXXIV.

ON a trip to the West Indies we went via Thomasville, Georgia, and Jacksonville, Florida. At the former place we stopped for a fortnight's shooting. This section of Georgia is slightly rolling, the soil sandy, and the country covered with extensive pine forests. Georgia produces more yellow pine than any other Southern State. The collecting of turpentine is one of the important industries of the people. The bark is removed from the trees for a space of six inches by thirty, and at the bottom a cup-shaped incision is made, into which the turpentine settles. The trees will stand tapping for five years, after which they become worthless for turpentine. It takes eight barrels of the crude fluid to make one of pure turpentine, the residue being five barrels of rosin.

The principal crop is cotton, which is still king, and the usual yield is about half a bale of marketable cotton to the acre. It takes fifteen hundred pounds of the crude to make five hundred pounds of lint or ginned cotton. Sugarcane is raised to some extent, and is manufactured into syrup for home consumption. Rice is also cultivated in small quantities. Peanuts are grown in profusion, and the places where they are planted are called "pindar patches," some of which are planted especially for the pigs to feed in. Corn is not a profitable crop, the yield being only ten or twelve bushels to the acre, and of the nubbin kind. They raise neither wheat nor hay.

Among the fruits are oranges, bananas, pomegranates, guava, and figs. Large quantities of citrons, watermelons, and sweet-potatoes are raised, and find an early market in the Northern cities.

Land is worth from five to ten dollars per acre, with the rattlesnakes thrown in. They have very tight and high fences, many being ten and twelve rails high and not staked; they are "horse-high, pig-tight, and bull-strong."

Red foxes are very scarce, but gray ones are abundant; the latter do not make as good a hunt as the former, taking soon to the fence or tree, because they have not the same endurance as the red variety. The latter are said not to be natives of America, but to have been imported from Europe before the Revolution, as they gave more excitement in the chase· Hunting the wild-cat is a sport that is very common in this section. They are generally pursued on moonlight nights. On one occasion while hunting with three or four dogs, we jumped quite a large cat in the timber. A peculiarity of this animal is that it never raises its head until there is an obstacle to surmount. We had taken our position on a log; soon the cat came slowly trotting toward us. Allowing him to approach within twenty or thirty yards—which we judged to be about killing distance—then raising our gun, there was a flash, a report, and his marauding career was ended.

Quail are plentiful, and with a good pair of dogs and a fair shot a bag of thirty could be easily made in a day. When we were going out several small boys made their appearance, and one asked Thomas W. Marshall: "Does you Yankees want we 'uns to mark and tote de game for you 'uns?" We engaged a half dozen at wholesale prices. They marked well, but "toted" few. Beside quail there are large flocks of blackbirds, robins, and doves, which every spring migrate north to breed. The mocking-bird is everywhere; it does not sing in the winter, but when spring returns and revivifies the earth with verdure and flowers, then this graceful bird fills the air with its voice, which is as sweet and varied as the multitudinous songsters of the groves. As Audubon says, "the mellowness of the song, the varied modulations and gradations, the extent of its compass, the great brilliancy of execution, are unrivalled. There is probably no bird in the world that possesses all the musical qualifications of this king of song, who has derived all from Nature's self."

The colored people are here to stay, and appear to be doing well. Many own farms, and with industry and a pair of mules make their fields white with cotton, and turn dirt into gold. They do not take much interest in politics, saying: " Politics won't make cotton, corn, and pork." We, however, differed with them about the *last article.*

Georgia is one of the most advanced of the Southern States. Railroads are being built, and the whistle of the locomotive can be heard at almost every point. Factories, saw-mills, and industrial establishments are springing up in all directions. The Georgia "cracker" does not seem to realize, as he lolls in the warm sun and watches the buzzard swinging in the soft air, between the tops of the green pines and the blue sky, that his country may, eventually, be one of the most prosperous States of the Union.

Leaving Thomasville we went to Jacksonville. It is quite a different place now to what it was when we were stationed there during the war, as Surgeon of the Ninety-seventh Regiment of Pennsylvania Volunteers, commanded by Col. Henry R. Guss. Now it has a population of ten or fifteen thousand, street-cars, and other modern improvements, and has become a great winter resort for Northern people. In winter the daily arrival of visitors is enormous. On the site of our old regimental hospital there is a splendid hotel. We made a trip up the St. John's River to the town of Enterprise. The river is sluggish, and cattle were observed standing in it, putting their heads at intervals under the water in search of a peculiar grass of which they are fond. Orange groves are plentiful along its banks, and the golden fruit shone through the green leaves, making one forget that it was winter. Alligators basked in the sun, while cranes and red flamingoes walked with dignity through the marshes as if they owned the soil. We also witnessed a contest between an eagle and a fish-hawk. The hawk was fishing along the river, and the eagle, knowing his object, followed him at a striking distance, but secluded himself among the trees. The hawk made several unsuccessful dives, but finally succeeded in catching quite a large fish. Then the eagle's opportunity arrived, and, allowing the hawk to get clear of the trees, he made a rush under him and kept him over the bed of the river. He drove the hawk up until they both appeared no larger than pigeons. Satisfied that he was at the proper elevation, he opened battle in earnest, and soon some feathers came floating down, for it was a rough-and-tumble fight in the air. It was fish or no dinner. The savage and dexterous attack of the eagle compelled the hawk to drop his prey. Closing his wings tight to his body, the eagle dropped like a thunderbolt and caught the fish in his talons just as it was striking the water. Then the *proud* emblem of America flew to one of the tallest trees in the forest, where he quickly devoured his booty, apparently satisfied that "to the victor belong the spoils." At Enterprise there are numerous mineral springs, and three kinds of water could be drunk within a few yards of each other.

From Jacksonville we embarked for Nassau, New Providence, the capital of the Bahama Islands, and a colony of England. In the time of the Revolution Admiral Esek Hopkins sailed from Philadelphia with a squadron, captured Nassau, and carried off the governor, eighty cannon, and a large quantity of ammunition, which were very beneficial to our cause at that period. Nassau has an equable temperature, both day and night, the thermometer registering about seventy degrees. All the tropical fruits grow here. The banyan tree with its branches grows downward into the ground, and the silk cotton tree will shade a thousand people. The harbor is about three miles long and from thirty to eighty feet deep, the water being as clear as the air. It is great sport to see the natives diving for coin. When a vessel arrives scores of these half-clad negroes swim around the vessel and beg the passengers to throw out money. As soon as it strikes the water away go half a dozen to capture the prize. You can see the silver shimmering in the water until it is caught. The process in repeated until the demand exceeds the supply. It is said that the whites are shy of diving, as they are too conspicuous, and the sharks "love a shining mark." The bottom of the harbor is of a bright greenish hue, and the effect produced is beautiful and deceptive. To the stranger, looking down into the depth of water, it does not appear to be more than five or eight feet in the deepest part. Along Hog Island, which is the bathing ground, many a novice jumps from a boat, expecting to get a footing at three or four feet, but he goes that many yards below the surface without touching bottom. The entrance to the harbor is defended by two forts, and the depth of water on the bar will admit vessels drawing fourteen feet. The sea-garden is a wonder; on the bottom can be seen miniature castles and grottos composed of coral and sponge, with fish as beautiful as humming-birds, darting around the shells, which shine like pearls. On the banks of the harbor are tons of coal and cinder, which were left by the blockade-runners, as this port was one of the great resorts for contraband traffic during our late war. Here vessels coaled and were loaded and unloaded with goods of every kind, from wearing apparel, provision, and medicine to ammunition and cannon; returning from the Southern ports they brought cotton. These vessels ran into Charleston, Wilmington, Savannah, and Mobile.

The lookout of Blackbeard, the pirate of the old buccaneer days, still stands, as does his old pirate fort. A mile to the west of Nassau is a beautiful cave, also called after the celebrated freebooter. In it, the natives say, he had much of his treasure hidden, and, though they appear to believe that it contains a great amount of wealth, they will not make an effort to recover it for fear that it will bring some calamity on the island. Several attempts were made to dig in the cave, but as soon as the pick and shovel were put in operation the groans and moaning were so appalling that the work was abandoned. It is probable that this noise was simply the echo.

The streets of Nassau are cut out of the solid rock, and rise terrace-like from the shore to the height of several feet. The island is of coral formation; on the north it is barren, but on the south and west it is fairly productive. Half the population are happy and lazy negroes. They are the police and magistrates, and generally run the local affairs. A garrison of white soldiers and a colonial governor are always stationed on the island.

## CHAPTER XXXV.

HAVANA, the capital of Cuba, was full of strangers at the time of our arrival, as it was the week of the carnival. Churches and amusements were well attended. The natives went to the former in the morning, in the afternoon to bull and cock-fights, and at night to mask-balls. The Plaza de Armes, the square on which the captain-general's palace is situated, reminded us of Paris, so brilliantly was it lighted, and enlivened with music by the governor's band.

The Paseo de Isabel, named in honor of Isabella I., is one of the finest streets in the city, laid out with walks, carriage drives, and several rows of trees. There is a large statue of the queen in the square at the head of the park, where a military band plays national airs every evening. Another handsome street is La Reina, or Queen Street, on which are the botanical gardens. At the corner of Empedrada and San Yanacio streets is the old cathedral, built of dark-colored stone, but now so old that it is almost black. It was built in 1724, and in it are the remains of the great navigator, Christopher Columbus.

He died at Valladolid, Spain, in 1506, aged seventy years. In 1513 his body was taken to Seville, and deposited in the family vault of the Dukes of Alcala. In 1536 the remains were conveyed to Santo Domingo, where they rested until 1796, when they were finally disinterred, and removed to Havana. Over his tomb is a niche in the wall, in which is his marble bust. All the churches in Havana are filled with life-sized paintings of celebrated persons and saints; the music is good, and the lepers sit at the church doors asking alms from those who go in or come out.

The private residences are all barred like prisons, whether to keep the proprietor in or the robber out, is not known. As Cuba is always very warm, white clothing is almost constantly worn by the adults, and, as for the little children, they were not troubled with bad-fitting clothes.

There are forty thousand soldiers on the island to look after the claims of Spain, and to keep the "patriots" quiet. We visited the noted fish-market where fish are sold alive, being kept in large tanks. The market bears the name of Tacon, who was the most enterprising captain-general that ever governed the island. The name was given to the market by a noted smuggler and pirate, named Marti. He had been outlawed by Tacon, who had offered a large reward for his capture. There is a story current that, after the reward had been published, Marti, one night, appeared at the palace of the captain-general, and having managed to evade the guards, succeeded in reaching Tacon's room without being seen. An interview took place between the outlawed smuggler and the governor, at the close of which the pirate went forth with a pardon for himself and companions, and a concession to build a fish-market, of which he was to have the control for ten years, when it was to become the property of the government. He named the market in honor of his patron. At the expiration of the ten years, he entered into another contract to build the famous Tacon theatre upon the same conditions.

Cows are driven through the streets with

# By Boat and Rail. 193

their calves tied to their tails, and are milked for the customers at their doors, thus insuring a pure supply of the lacteal fluid. Small horses carry stores on their backs, with glass cases and panniers so large that the rider has to take hold of the horse's tail to mount, and then sit cross-legged over the animal's neck. They have some fine Andalusian horses, and the riders sit the saddles admirably.

The *volante* is the national vehicle, resembling our old-time gig with its high wheels; the shafts are very long, and the horse is several feet from the dashboard, so far, that, if the animal kicked, its heels would not reach the occupants. The driver is really a rider, for he is mounted on one of the horses attached to the vehicle.

Tobacco is one of the principal products of the island,—sugar being the first. The finest plantations are west of Havana, in that district known as the Vuelta Abajo, where the best tobacco in the world for making cigars is raised. Not only do the men smoke, but also the women and children indulge in the luxury. You may get a very good cigar for five, or a very bad one for ten cents.

## CHAPTER XXXVI.

BEFORE leaving Cuba we visited Matanzas, which is sixty miles east of Havana and connected with it by a railroad. On the route we passed sugar and tobacco plantations, fields of pine-apples, groves of bananas, cocoanuts, and graceful palms. The houses are thatched, and the planters scratch the soil with a wooden plough drawn by oxen yoked by their horns. We saw herds of small horses, cattle, and goats, and flocks of game chickens. Matanzas is built upon a bay of the same name, which is formed by the San Juan and Yumarri rivers. The city is much like New York in point of maritime location. The harbor is one of the best in the West Indies. The streets are choked with trade, dust, and heat. The population is about forty thousand.

Securing a *volante* drawn by two horses, and a postilion riding one to urge the other, we rumbled along the rocky road at a flying pace until we reached the glittering caves of Bellamar, which are about three miles from Matanzas. The cave is entered by a stairway. The first apartment, which is called the "Gothic Temple," nearly two hundred feet long and about seventy-five feet wide, is iridescent with crystals of every hue, which are dazzling and beautiful. There are a number of smaller rooms with glittering stalagmites and stalactites, making quaint forms, to which have been given such names as "The Mountain," "The Mantle of Columbus," "The Guardian Spirit," "The Petticoat," "The Sacred Altar," and "The Cloak of the Virgin." " The Fountain of Snow" is a most agreeable feature of these forms. This cave, although grand, cannot be compared to the cave of Luray.

Returning to Matanzas, the drive took us through the lovely valley of Yumarri, named after the river which winds through it. The houses were all white, with tiled roofs. From Matanzas we returned to Havana, where we witnessed a *bal masque*, at which the participants appeared in fantastic costumes, black masks, and blacker eyes. The dance was slow and well timed by the beautiful *señoritas;* and when we left the ball, the watchman, with lantern and spear, was telling how goes the night.

The Tacon theatre, which has already been referred to, has a seating capacity of three thousand. There is a very good rule observed at this theatre, which might be adopted in other places, to wit: the manager is required to give first-class performances, to insure which an officer of the government is always on hand, and if he discovers that the play is being badly or indifferently rendered, he arrests and fines the manager.

Our stay in Havana having been completed, we embarked on the *City of Alexandria* for Mexico, and soon were passing under the sombre-looking El Morro, with its continually tramping sentinel, while the vesper bells were ringing as we bade adieu to the " Gem of the Antilles." El Morro is on the right as you pass out of the harbor, and on the left is La Punta, while back on the highlands, overlooking El Morro, is the immense fortress La Cabañas. These three are the guardians of the city. After sundown no vessels are permitted to enter or leave the port until sunrise the next day.

Passing through the narrow channel of the harbor we steamed away for Yucatan and Vera Cruz. On the way we stopped at the town of Progresso, one of the principal ports on the north coast of the peninsula of Yucatan, at which we left a cargo of corn, flour, and iron, and in return received sisal-hemp. Everything is lightered to and from the steamer, as they have no wharves. The native Indians are still numerous, and wear sandals tied to their feet by straps running between their toes. The men carry heavy loads on their backs, which are supported by bands around their foreheads, while the women sell fruit and get fat by sitting still. Merida, about twenty-two miles inland, is the capital of Yucatan, where all the merchants live who transact their business in Progresso. The streets are not named, nor do they designate their houses by numbers, but base the locality upon a street corner which has been given a name; for instance, the "Corner of the Duck," or the "Corner of the Elephant," and then say: "Our place of business, or residence, is the second door from the left of the 'Corner of the Duck.'"

The trip from Havana to Vera Cruz was

pleasant, as the winds were favorable and the gulf smooth. There were about seventy-five passengers, representing various conditions and countries—the Mexican with his head thrust through his poncho, the tightly clothed dandy from Paris, the olive-hued and black-eyed Cuban girl, and the high-heeled and bejewelled damsel from the States. This steamer was built by John Roach, the great shipbuilder of Chester, Pennsylvania, and was twenty-five hundred tons burden. It made fifteen knots an hour, and burned forty tons of coal daily. All the appointments were excellent, such as swinging-berths, barber saloon, bath-rooms, good fare, and polite officers. On the passage we saw but few vessels, but sharks, devil-fish, and flocks of flying-fish were abundant.

Vera Cruz, as we steamed into the harbor, looked beautiful with its white and blue domes, but it is a "whited sepulchre." It is built in the shape of a crescent, facing upon the gulf. There are a number of churches and a cathedral, built in the old Spanish style. The court-house and the prison adjoining, situated on an open plaza, are very imposing in appearance, and the pavements around them are tesselated. The people are not given to hard work, as horse-racing, chicken-fighting, and gambling appear to be the order of the day.

There is a strong wall around the city, and the fort, San Juan d'Ulloa, which is upon an island about a half mile from the shore, is its means of defence. Here, after a bombardment of seven days, General Scott landed during the Mexican war, and with his victorious army marched into the city. Now, there are about sixteen thousand inhabitants. The hotels are poor, the harbor uncertain and dangerous, and the drainage horrible, which make the town a pest-hole for yellow-fever and other diseases. Buzzards seem to be the only scavengers, and here you may see the curious anomaly of a boy, dog, and buzzard fighting for the same bone. The country around is sterile and uninteresting. There is a railroad two hundred and seventy-five miles long, connecting Vera Cruz with the city of Mexico, which was constructed and is operated by English capital. It is a wonderful piece of engineering, as it passes over and through mountains until it reaches an altitude of ten thousand feet. The scenery is like that of the Alps and the Yosemite, neither of which surpasses it in beauty or grandeur. You can look down upon clouds, trees, and cultivated valleys, while Mount Orizaba, seventeen thousand feet above the sea, looms up seven thousand feet above the track. It is an extinct volcano, seventy miles from the coast and visible for miles at sea. It is capped with perpetual snow and surrounded by fields that are always green. Three distinct climates are experienced in a single day. There is the blossom and the fruit, the green grain and ripe ear, and flowers in continual bloom. Corn, coffee, tobacco, wheat, sugar-cane, rice, bananas, oranges, and apples grow almost side by side. It is always seed-time and harvest in Mexico.

After leaving the mountains and the valleys, the road strikes the plains, which are of a loamy soil, and produce grain in abundance. Wood and water are scarce. Immense flocks of sheep and herds of cattle may be seen, with shepherds and dogs tending them, and gay horsemen swinging in the saddle, as they throw the lassos over the horns of the straying cattle.

## CHAPTER XXXVII.

AS you approach the city of Mexico, you see long lines of donkeys with loads larger than themselves, and four horses abreast drawing wagons with solid wooden wheels, the creaking of which can be heard for miles. The hay and fodder stacks are models of agricultural architecture, having crosses worked on their gables, and being impervious to the elements. Soldiers are on guard at each station to protect passengers and property from sudden invasion, as robbers here are not like angels' visits.

The olive-skinned women and darker men are anxious, with voice and gesture, to sell fruit and wares at every stop. The native men are to be seen with huge sombreros, pistols, and knives, incessantly rolling tobacco in cornhusk, which they smoke continually, and passing the greater part of the day dreaming of love and revolution. We passed many miles of maguey plants, from which the natives extract the *pulque*. This is the national drink, and is collected by tearing out the inner leaves of the plant, and making a cup-like receptacle into which the juice settles. It is then sucked by the natives into a long gourd, transferred to skins, and afterwards emptied into hogsheads. Special trains convey it from the country into the city, the railway company receiving thousands of dollars daily for its transportation.

The people of Mexico are very superstitious. It is told of them that, when the first steam-threshing machine was brought into the country, they were inquisitive as to its mode of operation and the source of its power. The machinist in charge told them that the devil was inside. The next morning he found a great number of wooden crosses around the machine, and when he inquired what they were for, the people said, "to keep the devil in." At night, all of the stock on the *haciendas* are driven into an enclosure, which is surrounded by a high and strong wall to protect the animals from thieves. Some of these Mexicans are exceedingly wealthy. One of them, whose *hacienda* had been raided by brigands, on being asked if he had sustained any loss, replied:

## By Boat and Rail. 203

"They took a mule-load of my kitchen silver only; my other service they did not find."

The city of Mexico has a population of three hundred thousand. The streets run at right angles. There are two beautiful streets, or *paseos* as they are called, which are wide and well paved. The Rio Paseo is on the west side, and the Paseo de la Véga on the east, both being embellished with fountains and statuary, and at night illuminated by electric lights. On many of the streets cars have been introduced. The police arrangements are admirable, and you are perfectly safe at all hours of the night. In some parts, which are not so well lighted, they place a lantern in the centre of the cross-streets, and if you wish an officer you will always find him in proximity to the lantern. The houses are well built of hewn stone of a light color, with roofs constructed of brick, and without chimneys, as they use charcoal for heating and cooking purposes. Some of the inhabitants live in luxurious style, and the appointments of their houses indicate prosperity. The churches, of which there are over sixty, under the exclusive control of the government, are objects of unusual interest.

The finest of the churches is San Domingo, but the most wonderful is the cathedral, which is built upon the ruins of the temple of the Aztec god. It is an immense structure, with elegantly carved and massive pillars and gilded images. The Church of Guadaloupe has an image of the Virgin, who is said to have appeared on the mountain. The people who are sick make pilgrimages to it, where they pray and drink the water, hoping to be healed of their infirmities. Although revolutions have torn the country into shreds, the soldiers of all factions have respected the shrine of Guadaloupe. The palaces, museums, and public buildings are filled with objects of interest. The national palace, formerly the residence of Cortez, the first viceroy, is now occupied by the President. Here also lived Iturbide and Maximilian, both of whom were emperors, condemned to death, and shot. The palace is covered on the inside with paintings of the generals, emperors, kings, and presidents of Mexico. Among them they have honored us by placing the portrait of General Washington. Here also are seen the silver-plate and the carriage of the unfortunate Maximilian, the carriage alone costing fifty thousand dollars.

The old aqueduct still supplies the city with water, but a new one is in course of construction. The city is below the level of the lakes, which makes it difficult to properly drain the streets. Mexico is so old that its history is a fiction, and the story of the Toltecs and Aztecs is written in rude characters on stone and in the crumbling ruins. Their pyramids, built of adobe, are still standing, and the sacrificial stone marks their cruelties. Their calendar stone, the idols which they worshipped, their instruments of war and peace, and their emblems of love are still to be seen. The "God of Death" is represented with a serpent in his girdle and corn in the palm of his hand, telling the old story, that no one escapes his grasp. We went to the once floating gardens, to reach which we were poled down the canal in a scow by a native Indian. This canal connects the lakes, which were once lined with palaces and thronged with business and pleasure. Now their greatness has gone, the gardens have sunk, and the onion supersedes the rose. On account of the high situation of the city there is no yellow-fever epidemic, as the fever only reaches a certain altitude.

The habits, dress, and customs of the people are almost the same as in Cuba and Spain, and many of the women are beautiful. In the afternoon the Paseo de la Véga is crowded with as elegant equipages as can be seen anywhere. The men sit their horses well, and both seem proud of their appearance. They carry enough gold and silver ornaments on their saddles and bridles to start a small circus. The Indians and donkeys appear to be the most active, though even they do not seem to hanker after work.

Labor is cheap, thirty cents a day being considered good wages. Any kind of seed that is put into the ground will reproduce itself. Fruit is abundant and costs but a trifle, consequently living is cheap. A blanket with a hole in it to put the head through is not expensive, yet we saw that the poverty of some of the inhabitants was so distressing that they did not even possess the cheap blanket. Lazarus would have blushed at their filth and sores.

The Republic of Mexico has ten or fifteen millions of inhabitants. It is rich in gold and

## By Boat and Rail. 207

silver mines, some of which have not been worked for three hundred years. There are mines eight miles long and over sixteen hundred feet deep, which, if properly worked, would annually produce twenty million dollars. The climate is perfect, the mercury standing at about sixty-five degrees the year around. The atmosphere is so pure that we saw venison drying in the sun.

Two and a half miles from the city is Chapultepec, the royal hill of the Montezumas. It is a rock of porphyry one hundred and fifty feet high, on the summit of which was the palace of the ancient kings of the Aztecs. It is now surmounted by a castle, and the fort of Molino del Rey is near its base. Both were stormed by General Scott before he entered the city of Mexico. Around the base of the rock are immense cypress trees, centuries old, some of them measuring fifty feet in circumference. A strong spring, gushing from the base of the hill, supplies the city with water.

The volcanoes of Popocatepetl, 18,500 feet high, and Iztaccihuatl are seen in the distance, the latter being so called on account of the perpetual snow on its top, which takes the form of a woman dressed in white. The tree, "Noche Trieste," is still standing, under the shade of which Cortez wept when he was driven from the city.

We visited the national pawn-shop, where we saw handfuls of diamonds and pearls and millions of silver dollars.

While in the city we witnessed a bull-fight, which was an exciting performance. The enraged animal, infuriated with fire and steel, made activity a necessity for his red-flagged tormentors, as he often grazed their buckskin breeches with his sharp horns and tramped their flags in the dust. On this occasion four bulls and as many horses were killed. It was a shocking sight to see the poor horses being spurred up to the fight, and the bulls goring out their bowels and tossing them in the air. Each act was terminated by the matadore, who, with a long sword and a red flag, stood in front of the bull, and, as the animal rushed at him, he plunged the sword with great dexterity into the nape of the neck. The animal staggered and fell, the blood gushing from its nostrils and mouth. The matadore bowed, and the four thousand spectators threw up their hats and fans and shouted at the slaughter. In the evening we saw excited crowds betting over bloody gaffs and dying chickens. It was a holiday of brutality and blood.

We stopped while here at a hotel which was built as a palace for the Emperor Iturbide. On the occasion of our visit to Mexico everything was going on well with the government, and revolutions and politics, like tallow, were quoted quiet.

# CHAPTER XXXVIII.

HAVING completed our visit to the Mexican capital, we returned to Vera Cruz and took steamer for New Orleans. The trip along the gulf coast was pleasant and without any incident of particular notice. It took five days to reach the deltas of the Mississippi. Captain Eads has made a wonderful improvement at the entrance of this river by his jetties. The channel, which was being constantly obstructed by the deposits of mud, has been deepened, so that now vessels of any draught may find a safe entrance and ascend the "Father of Waters" as high up as New Orleans.

The Mississippi is a wonderful stream and one of the longest in the world. With its tributaries it drains an area of a million and a quarter square miles. Nearly all the water between the Gulf of Mexico and British America, and between the Rocky Mountains and the Alleghanies, empties into it. Every year or so

## By Boat and Rail. 211

the country along its banks is inundated and millions of dollars' worth of property is destroyed. Various suggestions have been made by competent civil engineers, as to how the immense volume of water which is carried down this stream may be confined to its natural channel. Levees have been built, yet they have not resulted in any permanent protection to the planters. The floods raise the stream from twenty to forty feet above the lowwater mark. Recently our government had under consideration the construction of a series of canals to carry the overplus of water into other streams, and thus carry it back gradually to the river.

On our visit to New Orleans one of the most destructive floods that had ever devastated the country was in progress, and the river presented a turbid and uninviting appearance. On reaching the city we recalled to memory the days when General Butler was in full power, who proved a great benefactor to its people, by compelling them to keep the streets clean, and thereby preventing yellow fever from becoming epidemic.

The steamers which ply upon the river between New Orleans and St. Louis are floating palaces. They are large and roomy doubledeckers, brilliantly illuminated with electric lights. They are painted white and embellished with plenty of gilding. The trip was one of grandeur and excitement, as it was made during the flood. The country was completely submerged for miles on either side, and gave the appearance of an immense inland sea, only, instead of ships and boats, *débris* composed of trees, houses, and islands floated past. From one of these temporary floating islands our captain rescued a man, and another from an overturned dug-out. We did not keep to the river channel, but made short cuts across the bends, and frequently took up people, with their household effects, from some of the land which had not been covered. One evening a severe storm came on and the captain ran the steamer into a forest which was partially submerged and made fast to a big tree. As the boat forged along it broke down the smaller timber, which crackled like picket firing. We stopped at Vicksburg, Memphis, and some other points, but only long enough to exchange passengers and a little freight. At St. Louis we took the cars for the East.

## CHAPTER XXXIX.

IT was on a sharp, early spring morning when we steamed out of New York Harbor, on the steamer *Colorado*, bound for Rio Janeiro. The steamer had to touch at several ports before reaching its destination.

The first was St. Thomas, a rugged Danish island belonging to the Virgin group of the West Indies. The United States treated with Denmark for its purchase several years ago, but the two nations could not come to terms. It would have been a good investment for us as a coaling station.

Sugar-cane and a few vegetables are the principal productions. The capital is Charlotte Amalie, a city built on three hills, having a population of twelve or fifteen thousand, which is about the total population of the island. St. Thomas is chiefly noted as having been the rendezvous of the buccaneers who infested the West Indies two centuries ago.

On this island they had one of their lookouts, and the ruins of an old watch-tower are still to be seen. Here, also, Santa Anna took refuge when he failed in his attempts to become the absolute ruler of Mexico, and was obliged to leave the country. He had a residence in the country near the city of Charlotte Amalie.

St. Thomas is a free port and the principal coaling station for all American vessels bound along the South American coast; three thousand vessels annually visit it. The town is a hot place, full of negroes, Jews, and sailors. Our steamer lay there for about three hours, to exchange mails and passengers and to take in coal. It is not a healthy place, and the death-rate is high. The principal disease is consumption, caused by poor food and the miserable manner in which they generally live.

We took on board for "Rio" a French opera troupe, which had come from Mexico. They were pretty well done up, as the voyage had been a very rough one, consequently they were anything but musical, and their song was not of the sea. They had with them a great number of pets, and the *prima donna* had for her special amusement a monkey, on which she lavished her affections and jewelry, for it had diamond earrings and a gold necklace. There was nothing too good for its stomach. But there was a sudden termination to her love, for on one occasion the monkey, being irritable, made his teeth meet in her finger, at which she immediately snatched the jewelry from him and threw him into the sea, showing that there is but one step between love and hate, especially monkey-love.

From St. Thomas we stood away for Para, our first Brazilian port. To reach it we were obliged to cross "the line," which has been made so much of by sailors. The North Star, as we approached the equator, gradually disappeared in the north, while the Southern Cross, a grand constellation, became visible in the south. Under the equator the shadow cast by the sun is very small, that of your body not extending beyond your feet. The heat was intense, the mercury standing 96° in the shade, and by placing an ordinary Fahrenheit thermometer in the sun it burst in a short time. We also encountered the trade-winds, which blow from the northeast north of the equator, and from the southeast south of the equator. We saw sword-fish, dolphins, porpoises, sharks, flying-fish, and occasionally a whale. The flying-fish, from ten to twelve inches long, do not move their wing-like fins, but sail something like a flying squirrel. Several of them, in their flight, dropped on the deck of the vessel. Paradoxical as it may seem, sailors eat fewer fresh fish than any other class of people, as edible fish are seldom caught in fifty fathoms of water, generally keeping near the coast. The only bird we noticed was the stormy petrel, called by sailors Mother Carey's chicken, similar in shape and size to a barn-swallow, and the smallest web-footed bird. In the Orkney Islands, where it breeds, it becomes so fat that it is substituted for a candle by running a wick through its body. When they are seen in large numbers it is believed by mariners to be an indication of a storm. We passed the "Roccas," situated in the ocean about one hundred and twenty miles from Cape St. Roque. In bad weather they become an object of much anxiety to seamen.

In due time we reached the mouth of the great Amazon, which comes rolling through an almost uninhabited country. Its banks are covered with dense forests, which produce all kinds of medicinal and ornamental woods. Wild animals, serpents, and insects, the latter from the size of the minute "jagger," to beetles as large as a turtle, and birds of gorgeous plumage, inhabit them.

Lying right in the mouth of the Amazon is the Johannes Island. The left or northern arm of the river is the true Amazon, and the right or the southern branch is the Para, up which stream a distance of seventy-five miles is the city of Para. It is the chief trading port of Northern Brazil. The harbor is a capacious one, and vessels of the heaviest draught can find accommodation. The population is about forty-five thousand. The houses are white, with red-tiled roofs, which is very trying to those not accustomed to the glare of the red and the reflection of the white.

Para was founded in 1616. The climate is agreeable, although an equatorial city. In the forenoon it is hot, but towards evening a cool sea breeze springs up, generally accompanied by a shower, which purifies the air and cleans the streets. The water for drinking purposes, which is brought from springs situated in the country, is carried around in barrels on a wagon, and sold for a small sum per gallon.

The chief export is india-rubber, all the rubber from South America being shipped from this port. It is gathered with but little labor. The milk of the tree is collected by the Indians, which is colored dark by smoke, and then rolled into balls about a half foot in diameter. In addition to rubber, dye-woods, cocoa, tobacco, and coffee are exported.

Leaving Para, we sailed for Pernambuco, located on an ample bay, well protected from the ocean by a reef. The city has a population of about one hundred and thirty thousand. The streets are well constructed. This city is the great sugar mart of Brazil. A walk around the sugar warehouses is interesting. The sugar can be seen oozing through the bags, liquefied under the great heat of the sun, and actually running into the streets in rivulets. A ride was taken for several miles into the country, which carried us into the domain of lively monkeys and brilliant parrots. There are many old Portuguese customs still observed in this city. People are yet carried around in the

## By Boat and Rail. 219

sedan-chair, probably the only place where it is used outside of China.

From Pernambuco our steamer took us to Bahia, the oldest city of Brazil, situated on All-Saints Bay. The harbor is lighted by a revolving light, which can be seen on a clear night twenty-five miles at sea. Bahia has about one hundred and forty thousand inhabitants, and is divided into two parts. The lower town is on the bay, where all the trade is carried on. The upper town is several hundred feet above the lower, and is reached either by a number of zigzag paths, with steps cut into the rock, or by an elevator. The view from the upper town is grand. The bay is one hundred miles in circumference. The streets, though undulating, are well paved. A French company has undertaken the contract to properly drain the city, and has introduced waterworks. Making cigars, shoes, and cotton fabrics are the principal industries. The natives here have a curious nautical craft, called the catamaran, consisting of several logs lashed together and a sail. On this frail raft they brave the rough waves and winds in their occupation of fishermen.

From this port our voyage to Rio Janeiro

was exceedingly monotonous and oppressive. For days we did not see a sail. There was nothing but the sky, the ship, and the sea. At night the wake of the vessel could be traced by the sparkling light caused by the phosphorus and animalculæ in the water; and to the southward could be seen the "Magellanic Clouds," which appear like two thin and white clouds, but in reality are composed of numerous stars, clusters, and nebulæ.

## CHAPTER XL.

IT requires about three weeks, including the stops, to make the trip from New York to Rio Janeiro, the distance being about 5,500 miles.

Rio, as the city is usually called by seamen and those trading in South America, is the capital and chief city of Brazil, having a population of nearly four hundred thousand. It is situated on a magnificent bay, eighteen miles long and twelve, wide, and has frequently been compared with the Bay of Naples. The entrance to the harbor, which is a mile wide, is defended by two fortresses, Santa Cruz and St. Joan. On approaching the harbor, the first object seen is Sugar-Loaf Mountain, which looms up on the left; off to the southwest are the Corcovado Mountains, where they procure the water-supply for the city. This mountain resembles a man in a reclining position. The "Gavia," or Top-Sail Mountain, is another high point of land which appears like an immense sail. After passing the Narrows, on either side of which are located the forts, the bay widens; on the left bank is the city, and farther up a number of picturesque islands.

There were no wharves at Rio until within a few years. The late John Roach, of Chester, Pennsylvania, made a proposition to Dom Pedro, that, if the Brazilian government would give him the grant, he would construct wharves at his own expense, stipulating that he was to receive the revenues therefrom for a specified time, at the expiration of which they were to become the property of the government. The old Emperor declined the proposition, as he feared that it would deprive a large number of people of their occupation, viz., the loading and unloading of vessels. The government has, however, in later years done that which they had previously declined.

Rio is a very hot city, almost continually subject to yellow fever. This epidemic is largely due to imperfect drainage, and the neglect of sanitary regulations. The streets are quite narrow, some of them being so contracted that carriages cannot pass each other. There is a law governing the course of vehicles;

## By Boat and Rail. 223

finger-boards are placed upon the houses, similar to our pointer-boards, and no one is allowed to drive in an opposite direction to the index.

The "old town" is separated from the new by a handsome square, called the Campos de Santa Anna, which extends entirely across the city. This park is artistically adorned with statuary, fountains, stately palms, myrtle, and fragrant orange and lemon trees. It is the favorite resort of all classes, and in the evening a fine orchestra, under the pay of the government, entertains the people with national airs. The "new town" is built back upon the high lands. Its streets are well paved, the houses substantial, and constructed principally of granite.

As the late Emperor was an enthusiastic patron of whatever tended to advance the interests of the city and to benefit the people, there are large libraries, well-conducted charities, numerous benevolent institutions, colleges, and military and naval schools,—the result of his public spirit.

Every Brazilian citizen who is twenty-five years of age has a right to vote, and all who have an income of one hundred and twenty-five dollars a year are eligible as electors. The people are over-burdened with taxation; everything is taxed, even to a business sign.

In the principal business streets some strange sights are to be seen—for instance, long processions of negroes, some carrying bags of coffee on their heads, others pushing heavily loaded two-wheeled wagons over the cobble stones, and others moving in gangs of four, six, or eight, with their loads suspended between them on heavy poles. The mule is a much-respected animal in Brazil, as he is protected by the law from the lash.

The windows of the stores glisten with diamonds and precious stones, that can be bought cheap in the rough state. Some stores are entirely devoted to the sale of animals, birds, and reptiles. Beautiful artificial flowers are made from the feathers of birds, so exquisite that they charm the women and deceive the bees. Large numbers of monkeys, parrots, birds of beautiful plumage, and anacondas are shipped annually to the United States and Europe. A minute monkey, called the marmoset, is a great pet in the household, as he

# By Boat and Rail. 225

amuses the children, and performs the duties of a fine tooth-comb.

Electric light and gas have been introduced. The omnibus is fast disappearing, and the street-car is taking its place.

While in Rio we visited Petropolis, located in a valley in the Organ Mountains. To reach it you take a steamboat at Rio, and after an hour's ride you reach Maua, the terminus of the first railroad built in Brazil. The road is ten miles long, and takes you to the foot of the mountain, where coaches, drawn by six mules, carry you up to Petropolis, over a road that is not surpassed by any public highway. This road was built by the government for the Transportation of coffee, sugar, and minerals to the coast. The side of the mountain is so steep that three windings are compressed into a very small space. The surroundings and scenery are all that can be desired, and the climate is salubrious. Here the citizens retire in warm weather to be free from the heat, stench, and fever of the city. The town is garnished with villas and delightful gardens, and mountain streams run through the streets. Here the Emperor had his summer residence, to which he retired when the revolution occurred, which resulted in his abdication and the establishment of the Republic.

In this locality are some of the famous coffee plantations. The trees are not permitted to grow higher than twelve feet. The berry, when ready for harvesting, is about the size and color of a cranberry and contains two seeds. There are three gatherings in the year. The blossoms are white and exhale a delightful fragrance. But their beauty is short-lived, for the snowy flowers and odor last but for a day.

Coffee is a native of Abyssinia, and was introduced from that country into Arabia, and thence into Java. The Dutch governor-general of the latter country, in 1690, took a plant to Holland, where it was reared in a hot-house at The Hague. Some of these berries were sent to Surinam, and are the source of all the coffee in America. The first coffee-plant cultivated in Brazil was in 1774 by a Franciscan monk.

The transportation of the coffee to market is a business generally carried on by the natives. Each train, composed of thirty or forty mules, is arranged with the head of one mule tied to

## By Boat and Rail. 227

the tail of the one in front of him, and as the long procession winds down the mountain side, with bells tingling and the shouts of the drivers,. it affords a novel and interesting sight.

The stingless bees are one of the singular freaks of nature in this country. They make a sour honey, of which the natives are very fond.

## CHAPTER XLI.

IT was a blustering day in the month of March that we left New York on the steamer *Trinidad* for the Bermuda Islands. It requires about seventy hours to make the voyage. It was a rough passage, and only six passengers were at the breakfast-table the first morning out. The temperature of both the air and water increased as we travelled southward. North of the gulf stream the temperature of the air was 56°, of the water 54°. In the stream the temperature was: air, 76°; water, 72°; and at Bermuda, air, 68°; water, 72°; the average temperature at the islands is 75°.

Bermuda is about seven hundred miles south of New York, and six hundred miles directly east from Charleston, South Carolina, in latitude 32. The group is composed of 365 islands, only four of which are of any size. The largest, called Bermuda, is fifteen miles long by two, wide; the next, St. George, is three and a half,

## By Boat and Rail. 229

long and half a mile wide; the other two, Ireland and Somerset, are three miles long and less than half a mile wide. The others continue to decrease in size until they become merely coral rocks, standing up like points in the ocean. The population is about fourteen thousand, more than half of whom are blacks. There are two good hotels, the "Princess," at which we stopped, and the "Hamilton." The islands are divided into nine parishes, named after English noblemen. The entire group is of coral formation. The scenery is diversified and picturesque, and the country very hilly. As in all semi-tropical countries there is an excessive growth of verdure and a great variety of trees, the most noticeable being the palm. There are ten or a dozen different kinds of palms on these islands, varying in size from the little palmetto to the royal palm which grows to the height of sixty or seventy feet before it has a limb, the trunk having the appearance of granite. The other trees are the *avacado* or alligator-pear, the curious calabash tree, the tallow-tree, the cocoa-nut, and the wild coffee. Of plants there is an immense variety. The products are onions and potatoes, thousands of tons of which are sent in the early spring to New York, for which good prices are obtained in the markets of the principal cities of the States. There are a few banana and other tropical fruit-trees, which are chiefly raised for home consumption. Another article of export is the Bermuda lily, so much admired by floriculturists.

A large number of birds make these islands a casual resting-place in their migration north and south, and the islands are the eastern limit of their flight.

In the list of birds may be mentioned the red-bird, bluebird, cat-bird, the sora, several varieties of warblers, humming-birds, and the English sparrow, which keeps pace with the spread of the English language. As the Bermudas are over six hundred miles from the nearest mainland, it is astonishing how such small birds as the ruby-throated humming-bird, indigo-bird, snow-bunting, vireos, bobolink, and the slow-flying rail bird can make such a long flight and locate these islands. Snakes and toads are total strangers, and, it is said, there is not one of these reptiles to be found on the entire group.

## By Boat and Rail. 231

The houses are built of a coral rock, sawed into square blocks. The roofs of the houses are of the same material, and constructed with a low parapet, so as to catch the rain-water. On the ground, large receiving tanks of stone are built, which are white-washed, being constructed on a slight incline and connected with reservoirs. This care of rain-water is a necessity, as the wells are brackish. The whitewashing is done to destroy any vegetable or fungus growth, which is constant and rapid, and renders the water impure.

There are several caves on the islands, which add to its other attractions, glistening with stalagmites and stalactites. The principal is Walsingham, on the north side of Harrington Sound. Near this cave the poet Tom Moore resided, while he was registrar of the colony. On the southwest side of the same sound is Neptune's Grotto. Another curiosity is the Devil's Pond, which is full of fish, and only fed when strangers pay for the exhibition. The keeper threw in some dead fish while we were there, and those kept in the pond became so ravenous that they made the water boil as they tumbled and fought for the food. They acted more like savage animals than fish. The keeper said that one day a small dog accidentally fell into the pond, and that was the end of his *tail*.

The roads are as smooth as a floor, and in many places cut out of the hard, white rock. There are over one hundred miles of this kind of road on these islands, free from dust, mud, and toll. There is an excellent yacht club, which often gives regattas. The Eagle's Nest, three hundred and fifty feet high, is the loftiest point on the islands, from which all the islands are visible, and the view of the ocean is complete in every direction.

The dockyards are located on Ireland. The floating dock, nearly four hundred feet long, was constructed in England, and towed over. It required two war vessels forty days to drag it across the Atlantic.

There is a strong fort on St. George's Island, which is garrisoned by an English regiment, and several British war vessels are always stationed here.

After a week of sight-seeing on the islands, we took passage back to New York on a steamer loaded with potatoes and onions, of which the latter made their presence known by their vigorous odor.

The second night out we met with a terrific storm. The elements appeared to have combined to destroy us. The savage wind and lashing waves struck our ship with such force that it seemed as if they would crack her ribs and crush in her iron sides. The steamer rolled and plunged, and trembled from stem to stern like an aspen leaf. With the rattling of the hail, the reverberation of the thunder, and the pelting of the storm, the night was appalling. The quick lightning played upon the curling waves, and illuminated the dark and deep-blue valleys of the surging sea. But when morning came, and the sun showered her golden light upon the ocean, it sparkled as if sprinkled with gems—

> " The air was calm, and on the level brine
> Sleek Panope with all her sisters play'd."

THE END.

www.ingramcontent.com/pod-product-compliance
Lightning Source LLC
Chambersburg PA
CBHW020809230426

43666CB00007B/931